THE LIVING ROOM SERIES

WHAT LOVE IS

The Letters of 1, 2, 3 John

kelly minter

LifeWay Press®Nashville, Tennessee

Published by LifeWay Press®
©2014 • Kelly Minter
Reprinted 2015

ISBN 9781430031550
Item 005635536
Dewey decimal classification: 248.84
Subject heading: CHRISTIAN LIFE \ LOVE \ BIBLE. N.T. JOHN (EPISTLES)

To order additional copies of this resource, write LifeWay Church Resources Customer Service; One LifeWay Plaza; Nashville, TN 37234-0113; FAX order to 615.251.5933; call toll-free 800.458.2772; email *orderentry@lifeway.com;* order online at *www.lifeway.com;* or visit the LifeWay Christian Store serving you.

Printed in the United States of America
Adult Ministry Publishing
LifeWay Church Resources
One LifeWay Plaza
Nashville, TN 37234-0152

TABLE OF CONTENTS

PHOTO CREDIT: JULEE DUWE ROARK

For more information on the work Justice and Mercy International is doing around the world, check out justiceandmercy.org.

MEET THE AUTHOR

KELLY MINTER IS AN AUTHOR, SPEAKER, AND SONGWRITER. SHE IS PASSIONATE ABOUT WOMEN DISCOVERING JESUS THROUGH THE PAGES OF SCRIPTURE. SO WHETHER IT'S THROUGH STUDY, SONG, OR THE SPOKEN WORD, KELLY'S DESIRE IS TO AUTHENTICALLY EXPRESS CHRIST TO THE WOMEN OF THIS GENERATION. SHE HAS FOUND DEEP HOPE AND HEALING THROUGH THE BIBLE'S TRUTHS, MAKING HER MESSAGE PERSONAL AND RELATIONAL.

No Other Gods, the first installment of The Living Room Series, helps women unveil the false gods in their lives for the ultimate purpose of discovering freedom in the one, true God. *Ruth: Loss, Love & Legacy* follows the redemptive story of Ruth, displaying God's providence and purpose even in the most trying circumstances. *Nehemiah: A Heart That Can Break* is an unforgettable journey into the missional heart of God. All studies are presented in the same Living Room Series format (studies can be done in any order). Kelly also released her first memoir, *Wherever The River Runs: How A Forgotten People Renewed My Hope In The Gospel,* about her life-changing journeys to the Amazon jungle.

Kelly writes extensively and speaks at women's conferences and events around the country. She has her own event called Cultivate: A Women's Gathering Around The Word. This Biblically based and stylistically simple event is for women of all ages. Kelly also partners closely with Justice and Mercy International, an organization that cares for the vulnerable and forgotten in the Amazon and Moldova. Kelly's music includes *Loss, Love & Legacy,* which complements her Ruth study, and the worshipful *Finer Day.* To view more about Kelly's studies, books, music, and calendar, visit *www.kellyminter.com.*

INTRODUCTION

Out in the countryside of Northern Virginia, fathers smacked baseballs to the horizon and ran around bases, while moms smashed hamburger patties between buns and children tumbled down hills covered in hay. At a summer church picnic, everyone seemed as light as the clouds floating in the sky. Except, I was not floating. Fear had gripped me—something that not even a good roll down the hillside could shake. Paralyzing anxiety characterized parts of my childhood, and today was one of those days. I remember some calming words visiting me, though—words I must have memorized even earlier in my childhood. "Perfect love casts out fear." The phrase from 1 John 4:18 (NKJV) is my earliest recollection of God speaking to me from John's epistles. What did this mean, exactly? My 12-year-old brain wasn't completely sure. But right there in a sprawling field, the Lord began to take His sword to the giant I knew as Fear.

As a child I was often uncertain of my salvation. At night I'd contemplate eternity, comforting myself with more of John's words, "so that you may know that you have eternal life" (1 John 5:13). I'd stare at the ceiling in the hovering dark, reminding myself that John said we could know, but wishing I knew just a little more. Then there were the Sunday School songs we used to sing with graham crackers in our stubby hands, hardly understanding the weight of what we were proclaiming. "Behold what manner of love the Father has given unto us, that we should be called the sons of God" (3:1). Only we'd hold the "weeeeeeeee" out really long, and it always bothered me that I had to sing "sons" when I was clearly a daughter. As I grew older and guilt or doubts would overwhelm me I'd fall into that glorious phrase, "Whenever our heart condemns us, God is greater than our heart" (1 John 3:20 ESV). Who could dream up a line like that but John? Who could make it a reality but Jesus?

As life's lures and temptations became more complex and magnetic I heeded words such as, "Do not love the world" (2:15). I didn't know exactly what it meant to not love the world I lived in, but the Bible made it sound pretty serious. I had hoped this didn't include ice cream cones, but one could never be too cautious. Still, these cautions were tempered by unforgettable lines like, "We love because He first loved us" (4:19, HCSB) and "This is love: not that we loved God, but that he loved us" (4:10). John was laying the foundations of what I would later come to understand as theology.

In real estate terminology, John's letters do not enjoy the benefits of location, location, location. They're small, tucked back by the concordance, somewhere after Paul and before Revelation. While they're often quoted, full of bite-sized nuggets you can grab in a pinch, as a whole they aren't as well known. Furthermore, John's letters can be hard to understand. I've often struggled with him: *Why did you write that? What do you mean? Can you give this to me in layman terms?* Some of his words shake me to the core and in the next breath wash me with comfort. His warnings are fiery and his affirmations fatherly. Though his letters were written in another era, I've found his message squarely for today.

So whether you've come to these books because you already love John, are a fan of the notable verses, or have always wondered what those books near the back were about, I'm wholeheartedly ecstatic for you. Because I'm not sure if any other study has changed me so. John's themes of fellowship, light, assurance, abiding, and love are wonderfully grounding. And if you've ever heard words like *atonement, propitiation, incarnation* and thought they were only for smart, stuffy academics, you'll discover how the meanings of these words have the power to change all of life for us. John's heart is pastoral, his voice pleading. He's the coach who makes you stay after practice to run the bleachers, but only because he sees your potential. And his message couldn't be timelier.

In an age when opinions fly at us unbridled, John gives us the immutable gift of truth. When science and philosophy and your social circles say you can't really know God, John says, yes you can. Dear child, he continues, I've touched Him. Where we've not only settled for living in the gray, but have formed our identity in it, John points us to light and dark—you're walking in one or the other. And perhaps most importantly, at a time when the word *love* means just about anything under the sun, and therefore almost nothing, John tells us "this is what love is…."

And then he shows us Jesus.

Bread & Butter Pickles

2 gal. pickles sliced
3 Handfuls salt
4 tablespoonfuls mustard seed
2 tablespoonfuls celery seed
7 C. sugar
2 qts. vinegar. Mix ...

... come to boiling point ... over pickles. Reheat 2 or 3 times. Bring vinegar to ... point ... to a pint ...

THE FINEST INGREDIENTS

I once took a cooking class with a friend. We decided on an Italian class since *passami l'olio* (pass the olive oil) could be my life's motto in the kitchen. The instructor was an exuberant and portly woman who was big on personality and apparently on calories. I found this made her more believable—no one wants to eat the food of a skinny Italian. Before us lay piles of plum purple eggplants, sweet onions, and garlic, hunks of crusty bread and imported Romano cheese. Among the other delectable beauties were shiny Roma tomatoes, fresh basil leaves, bulbs of fennel, pancetta, ground veal and pork, live clams awaiting their fate on ice. We would be making *zuppa di vongole* (clam soup), *fette di melanzane ripiene* (baked eggplant and provolone), a salad with homemade dressing, and perhaps my all-time favorite, *ziti al ragu della nonna* (better known as pasta with grandma's meat sauce). Just reminiscing about this evening is sending me into a carb frenzy of cheeriness and warmth.

The eight of us went around the room and introduced ourselves, also sharing why we were interested in the class. Everyone pretty much gave the same response, which was some version of wanting to know how to better cook meat sauces and classic pasta dishes. (Except the one single fellow who said that male Italian cooks on television seem like really cool guys and learning to cook Italian might better his chances of meeting someone. So that was interesting.)

We made several dishes that night, paring vegetables, grating cheese, browning meat, making sure all the clams had opened their little shells assuring us they'd actually died while simmering in the sauce and not sometime earlier—this was as pleasant as it sounds. Our instructor frequently encouraged us to taste-test our various sauces as we went, adjusting seasonings and spices until we were delirious. Every spoonful was an eruption of flavors consisting of savory nuances that I couldn't quite pinpoint but that gave me a sense of home. (I know I have ancestors from Italy.)

Every time our chef crinkled the paper off a garlic bulb or diced the flat-leaf parsley, she'd explain the value of fresh herbs, whole imported cheeses, high-quality meats, trying out different onion varieties, using tomatoes from the vine, or at least ones that were canned during their peak (I had this one covered). She introduced new herbs into my repertoire, like saffron and ground fennel seed. And she explained the difference between pancetta and bacon—pancetta is cured, but not smoked, while bacon is smoked; subtleties that make a difference in your sauce. She minced garlic and shallots like her fingers were ballerinas, tossing them into a swirl of lemon juice, olive oil, and fine vinegar. "Good balsamic vinegar," she explained, "will be made from must only. Not caramel or vinegar." I was scribbling as fast as she was talking—that is, when I wasn't carrying on the all-important task of taste testing.

I was adamant about following her every move, but every time I turned around she was veering from the recipe, adding more of this or less of that, rummaging for ingredients that weren't even on the list in the first place. "It's not mentioned on your sheet," she'd say, "but do you know how good a hint of orange juice is in a red sauce?" Then she'd ask me to peel an orange and squeeze in an unmeasured amount of juice. The chef was killing me! I wanted step-by-step instructions on how to make a meat sauce that would make someone's Tuscan grandmother proud. I wanted people to cry at my dinner table and embrace one another for long periods of time. I couldn't accomplish this by having a mere "feel for things," a phrase she often used. Didn't she understand that I needed measurements, temperatures, tools, and pretty much for her to live in my pantry? But what I realized at the end of the evening was that she'd given me all I really needed: the ingredients.

When reading through the letters of John, especially 1 John, sometimes I feel like I'm back in that kitchen with a genius chef who doesn't use recipes. I find myself thinking things like, *Wait … what exactly do you mean by that?*, or *Could you tell me a little more?*, or *How many tablespoons of love and truth exactly?* But John doesn't always tell you. His letters are not step-by-step tutorials on how to work out that troubling relationship, what to do with your chronic addiction, how you can beat depression. We won't get much narrative out of him and sometimes we'll wish for more explanation. But what we will get are some of the finest ingredients of our faith: love, assurance, fellowship, purification, justification, propitiation, forgiveness, overcoming, knowledge, and so many more.

We'll find John slipping these tried and true doctrines into the sauce in new ways, or using lesser known ones that add a spice we've never before enjoyed. We'll nourish ourselves at the table of these biblical truths, taking our time with each ingredient. We'll further understand how the pure extract of the gospel can radically change our lives if we'll simply taste and see. I can't wait to begin this exploration with you. I have no idea the sauce we'll come up with in the end, but I can assure you we'll use the finest of the gospel's ingredients. They're the only kind John cooks with.

VIEWER GUIDE

INTRODUCTION

GROUP DISCUSSION QUESTIONS:

What do you hope to gain from this study and the time spent together?

How do you react to the idea that genuine love has substance and definition?

Which is most difficult for you to grasp or embrace: Jesus' complete humanity or divinity? Why?

John shares "that which was from the beginning." How does the eternal nature of the gospel ground you in a world that is fleeting and temporary?

In what ways do you struggle in a culture that often communicates that what a person believes doesn't matter, truth is ever-changing, or the gospel is narrow and confining?

How is believing in Jesus a progressive and dynamic process rather than a static past accomplishment?

PUTTING THE PIECES TOGETHER

Emmett and I sat on the hardwood floor of my parents' home in a pile of puzzle pieces. In keeping with his 4-year-old, red-headed zeal, Emmett jammed together whatever pieces were most convenient to his reach, happy to try one right after the other until two magically pressed together. As his oldest and most experienced aunt, I tried to teach him about corner and flat-edged pieces. I explained in the simplest of terms that if one could identify those corner anchors, then move on to assembling the border, hereby eliminating excess parts to contend with, and finally move on to grouping like pieces by color, imagery, and shape, the puzzle could be solved with ease and expedience (and I could get back to my morning coffee). Emmett looked at me like I was the ruiner of good times; I looked at him like, have you ever had French press?

In most areas of my life I share Emmett's propensity to circumvent pre-work in my excitement, tearing straight into a new project while tossing preparation and directions aside—I so like to get on with things. But when I begin studying a new book of the Bible I have a competing desire to get my bearings, to understand the context of the times, the history of the author. So today I want us to ready ourselves for 1, 2, and 3 John. We'll gather some corner pieces and find the borders of our study. The more we understand about John, the more his heart and message will emerge. While I can't guarantee every space will be filled or every piece will fit perfectly snug at the end of our weeks together, I have no doubt the overall picture will be impossible to miss.

To get a cursory feel for John's life, let's pull some biographical information together.

> According to Matthew 4:18-22 who was John's father and who was his brother?

> What can you deduce was John's occupation?

> According to Matthew 10:1-4, among which prestigious group is John named?

Sometimes I inadvertently split up certain characters of Scripture into several different people depending on what book I'm studying. For instance, I used to have a hard time keeping Mary of Bethany straight. Was she Martha's sister Mary who sat at Jesus' feet in Luke? Mary whose brother Lazarus had died in John? Mary who anointed Jesus' body with perfume in Matthew, Mark, and John? When I finally understood that yes was the answer to all of these I realized I had missed out on understanding the breadth of her story. (I find the number of Marys in the Bible downright challenging.)

I tend to do the same with John. There's John who wrote John's Gospel; John who wrote the letters 1, 2, and 3 John; John who penned Revelation. And, there's John who shows up in all the synoptic gospels (Matthew, Mark, and Luke) sometimes fishing with Peter and James, or running to the empty tomb, or even arguing about who will be first in the Kingdom. He appears in Acts and is mentioned in Galatians. Who knew these were all the same John?

My point is, when we study books of the Bible it's easy to unwittingly draw circles around each book or story, inadvertently freezing its characters in place. As we study John's epistles, I want us to keep our circles permeable, allowing for John the person—what we know about him from Scripture—to move freely in and out of his letters as we read them. I think we'll get the most from him and his message this way, and we'll keep his humanity more tangibly in mind. I'll help us do this as we go, frequently having us visit other parts of Scripture while offering historical insight. For now, let's grab some corner pieces by looking at a few key moments in John's life from a chronological perspective.

Note that John's brother James, one of Jesus' disciples, is different from the James who was Jesus' brother and the writer of the epistle James.

Luke 5:1-11 is one of John's earliest recorded encounters with the Lord. In verse 9, what strong adjective describes John's reaction?

❏ angry/furious
❏ overwhelmed/overcome
❏ sorry/repentant
☑ astonished/amazed

PERSONAL REFLECTION: Briefly name a time early in your relationship with Christ when Jesus amazed you. Remembrance is a beneficial discipline of our faith, so take time to think back.

Once we begin our study of John's epistles, these early encounters that John had with Jesus will mean even more to us. We'll discover that the church of John's day (possibly as much as 70 years after Christ's death) was in a crisis of belief because false teachers were undermining the truths of Christ's identity as both God and man. Understanding how closely John walked with Jesus and how deeply he knew Him will give deeper credence to his three letters. It will help us understand why he wrote with such passion and why he vehemently opposed those who opposed the truths about Jesus. John had known Him. Seen Him. Heard Him. Laid his head upon His breast.

> Read Mark 5:35-43 and briefly describe the desperate situation into which Jesus was called.
>
> Synagogue Ruler
>
> Which disciples did Jesus permit to come with Him?
>
> Peter, JAMES , and John.
>
> Reread verses 37 and 40 and check the number of people in the room:
>
> ☑ five   ❑ seven   ❑ eight   ❑ twelve

> **PERSONAL REFLECTION:** Consider the intimacy and emotion of this experience. How might this have impacted John's faith in Jesus? Briefly record a time when you experienced the Lord's presence in a particularly intimate way.

I don't know of anything more meaningful than when, in the middle of the commotion, God taps us on the shoulder, whispers our name, and welcomes us into the room where He's about to do something special, even secret. Is there a more sacred, more holy place of fellowship than being chosen by Him for a certain work? We tend to think God has invited someone else into the fold, someone nobler, more righteous, more gifted than we are. But Scripture as a whole tells us otherwise. Ephesians 2:8-10 speaks specifically to this.

One of my friends astutely said, "As the channels of social media grow we hear more and more about people doing 'amazing things'. We see how everyone else is leading these 'great lives'. In the Christian realm we feel our faith has to be at a certain level of depth before we can be used or make a difference." Even though the opportunities to draw comparisons are exponential right now—Facebook, anyone?—remember how the Lord calls each of us to our own unique race, just as He called a fisherman named John. One of the beautiful parts of having a relationship with Jesus is how personal and intimate it is. In John's Gospel we read about another significant encounter John has with Jesus that's as intimate an exchange as anything I can imagine.

> What significant responsibility did Jesus entrust to John at the cross? (See John 19:25-27.)

> What specifically did John do for Mary?
>
> *Took her into his home –*
>
> **PERSONAL TAKE:** What qualities and characteristics can we surmise John had for Jesus to have asked this sacred task of him?

Now that we've visited John in a few different settings with Jesus before the cross, let's look at a couple of mentions after Jesus' resurrection. We'll do this briefly. In Galatians 2:7-10, the Apostle Paul recounts an experience he had in Jerusalem.

> What interesting noun does Paul use to describe James, Peter, and John? (v. 9) *Grace given to Paul –*

> What did John and these men offer Paul?
>
> *Right hand of fellowship –*

I don't know why but I've never thought too much about Paul's and John's ministries overlapping. Again, for some reason I had John frozen in the Gospels and Paul in his epistles, forgetting that the two were contemporaries.

Perhaps what's most fascinating to me is that John outlived all the other original twelve disciples, even Paul. When John wrote his epistles, he was the last disciple remaining, something you'll be able to tell from the passion and urgency with which he writes. You'll be able to sense how desperate he is to proclaim and protect the purity of the gospel of Jesus as the last of the original voices of those who knew Him. If you're not yet hooked, look at one last text for today. Read John 20:1-9. Keep in mind how John's experience at the tomb will shape his letters we're about to study. Note that *the disciple Jesus loved/the other disciple* is widely presumed to be John.

When John entered the tomb (v. 8) it says that he saw and
believed .

This word has eluded me at different times in my life. Sometimes my belief is shrouded in doubt, sometimes it's overturned by blatant unbelief, at other times pain and suffering threaten to cut off its oxygen supply. Maybe this is why I love this passage so much.

Certainly John believed in Jesus before stepping into the tomb, but what we gather from the context is that he believed more fully what Jesus had been saying to him all along. This is my prayer for you and for me as we study 1, 2, 3 John—that we might believe! Whether you're a seasoned believer, taking your first steps with Jesus, or without faith at all, I can't wait to journey with you through these letters. As Martin Luther so eloquently said about 1 John: "It can buoy up afflicted hearts."[1] As we go, may we be buoyed both by seeing and believing.

DAY 2

WORD OF LIFE

Settle in. Do your best to put the concerns of the day aside and turn to 1 John. As you read, picture an aged man writing some of his last words to his beloved church. Envision the deep lines etched across John's forehead from his sun-scorching years as a fisherman, a disciple of Jesus, a pastor of the scattered churches at Ephesus. See his tenacious eyes that long to protect his people from the onslaughts of deception—he is the last of the twelve still living and the times are urgent.

For all John's tenacity, don't miss the love, the tenderness he has toward his "dear children," perhaps the same tenderness that prompted Jesus to entrust His mother Mary into John's care. And as you let the opening words of 1 John envelop you, most of all, notice who still remains at the center of this author's heart. Welcome to 1 John.

Read 1 John 1:1-2

Did you notice that John doesn't identify himself? He gives no formal greeting and no indication to whom he's writing. Though this is rare in ancient Hellenistic letters, strong evidence points to John's authorship.

> What unique title does John give Jesus in verse 1? The
> __*Word*__ of __*Life*__.

My friend Marcie likes to say that every verse in John's epistles is like a drop of perfume, a fragrance that invites you to breathe deep and linger. Given her wisdom, I'm inclined to explore the two words, *word* and *life,* for the rest of the day. But for fear of losing some of you who actually have agendas, we will pause for just a moment.

> Turn to John's Gospel and read verses 1:1 and 14 and fill in the blanks. (1) "In the beginning was the __*Word*__, and the Word was __*with*__ God and the Word __*was*__ God. (14) The Word became __*flesh*__ and made his dwelling among us."

> **PERSONAL TAKE:** Why do you think John refers to Jesus as the Word? Give this some thought even if you've never been given a formal explanation.

About John 1:1, A.W. Tozer said: "An intelligent, plain man, untaught in the truths of Christianity, coming upon this text, would likely conclude that John meant to teach that it is *the nature of God* to speak, to communicate His thoughts to others."[2] (emphasis mine.) The fact that one of Jesus' titles would embody the very essence of communication is one of the most welcoming and astounding of His qualities.

> **PERSONAL REFLECTION:** John begins his letter with the premise that the God he knows is a speaking God. How does this encourage you in a culture that often portrays Him as mysterious, silent, or unapproachable?

That one of Jesus' titles would embody the very essence of communication is one of the most welcoming and astounding of His qualities.

The word for *word* is *logos* and can be translated *word* or *reason.* It can even mean *revelation,* since Jesus is the revelation of the Father. *Word* is a beautiful and natural name for our Savior because He literally reveals the Father. Scholars debate whether John is referring to the Word as Jesus

Himself, or to the word as the life-giving message of Jesus.[3] The power of John's meaning is not lost either way. In many respects both the message and the person are the same, "For the life-giving word of the gospel is essentially a proclamation about Jesus who is the living Word of God."[4] Sometimes I have to remind myself how much God wants to be known.

As you noted earlier, in 1 John 1:1 John refers to Jesus not only as the Word, but also as the Word of Life. The word *life* is a favorite of John's. His writings are responsible for including 66 of the 139 mentions of the word in the New Testament—almost half, for all you math wizards.[5]

In the Gospel of John 1:2-4 and 5:26, what important preposition is used to describe Jesus' relationship to life?

❏ Life is with Him. ❏ Life is before Him.
❏ Life is beside Him. ☑ Life is in Him.

To put an even more personal touch on this, flip over to the Gospel of John 11 and ponder verse 25. This is Jesus speaking to Martha after her brother Lazarus had died. Who does Jesus tell Martha He is? I am the Resurrection and the Life .

My sister Megan and I talked on the phone last night about a long and hard situation that doesn't seem to be changing. We've prayed for God to do something, but Megan reminded me that when we can't see what He's doing, healing comes from remembering who He is. When Jesus met Martha in her hour of devastation and grief, He didn't tell her what He could do, rather He told her who He is—life itself.

First John 1:1 is the only time in the Bible the title *Word of life* is used. Consider all the options John could have plausibly written to describe Jesus in his opening verse: Word of love, Word of truth, Word of hope, Word of peace, Word of power. But He calls Jesus the Word of life, and this means something special to me.

I know that some women reading these verses right now are barely making it. Real women going through real suffering—women in hard marriages, women in hard singleness, women weighed down by shame or heartbreak or addiction, women desperately afraid that life may never change, women going through the motions who might describe themselves as lifeless. And here—in the opening verse—John describes Jesus as the Word of life. Dear reader, this is as grand an opening as we could hope for.

PERSONAL REFLECTION PART 1: Do you currently feel lifeless in any areas of your life? (Marriage, work, personal relationships, relationship with God, parenting, outlook, etc.) Don't worry about what you should say, just let your pen flow.

PERSONAL REFLECTION PART 2: Write a prayer asking Jesus to breathe His life into your situation. He has the ability to take what is barely breathing and revive it to wholeness. He can take what is dead and raise it to life, because He is the resurrection and the life.

What specific action did this "life" take in 1 John 1:2?

☐ vanished/disappeared   ☐ changed/was transformed
☑ appeared/was revealed   ☐ hid/was covered

What John is declaring here is the great doctrinal truth of the incarnation. Though this term is not actually found in Scripture, it describes a scriptural anchor of our faith: God came to us in human flesh. Or more precisely, the incarnation is "The act of God the Son whereby he took to himself a human nature."[6] John is declaring that the Deity, the one true God has come in the form of human flesh; He has appeared to us.

Your translations may use the word *manifested* or *revealed*. As we continue our study we will see why John makes such a point of establishing this important doctrine of God coming in flesh right at the top. But for now, take a moment to appreciate what it means for the Word of life to have appeared on this earth.

Near the end of verse 2, John throws out an additional adjective to further describe this revealed life. What is it?

☐ hopeful   ☑ eternal
☐ temporary   ☐ fleeting

How does Jesus describe this life in the Gospel of John 17:1-3?

eternal Life

The life that Jesus came to bring is so much more than simply living. But I wonder how much we really believe this? I still have moments when I feel like I've somehow missed the last train out of the town of Survival, watching all the happy people waving out the windows on their way to a honeymoon, the career path I've always dreamed of, an awards ceremony, to meet their first grandchild, or to the mall with money in their wallets. I think we sometimes consider having life in terms of physical, sensual, and emotional pleasure, and when we don't get it or can't have it we get angry or resign ourselves to a life of scraping by. We think God has failed us, or life is for all those other people on the train. John is going to plead with us to the contrary!

We tend to think of life in terms of what can be added to us, but one of the characteristics of having eternal life is the removal of something.

Read the Gospel of John 5:24-26, verse 24 says we will not be _Condemned_.

The Jews of Jesus' day thought that they could have eternal life by doing what (see John 5:39-40)?
Studying the Scriptures

Instead, what did Jesus say they needed to do to have life?
Come to Jesus

In John 10:7-10, what kind of life does Jesus say He came to bring?
- ☑ abundant
- ☐ spiritual
- ☐ comfortable
- ☐ burdensome

When I read about the Word of life in 1 John 1:1, I can't think of anything more hopeful than this reality—life is a Person. Life is not a career path or an attentive husband or a new home; it's not enlightenment or nirvana or a religious experience; it's not a degree or a philosophy. Life is Jesus, and anyone who comes to Him may have Him and all He offers. My prayer is that Jesus as the Word of life, the very expression of life, will pierce the reality you're living in, awaking your heart and soul to abundant living in Him. Jesus makes this possible.

DAY 3
WITH US

I might as well go ahead and get this out there: I've decided there's just no way to zip through 1, 2, and 3 John. They're not zipping kinds of reads. But taking our time doesn't mean slow as much as it means deep. Perhaps we can think of ourselves as scuba divers swimming down, as opposed to freestylers swimming across. We're going to cover depth as opposed to breadth. Or, if you prefer Marcie's perfume analogy, we'll allow ourselves the pleasure of time while smelling the individual scents throughout John's epistles. I find it helps if we can get ourselves into this kind of mindset, making it easier when I say: turn to 1 John and read verses 1-2—the same verses you read yesterday. (Remember the scuba diver. Or the perfume.)

> In what sensory ways did John have contact with Jesus (v. 1)?
> ☑ touched Him ❑ smelled Him ☑ heard Him
> ❑ knew Him ☑ saw Him

You may have noticed that instead of using the word *I*, John uses *we*, referring to those in Jesus' inner circle. John uses the *we* to establish the weight of his message, because he's not merely out to tell a story, he's "virtually swearing a deposition."[7] John said that he had heard Jesus, seen Him with his own eyes, touched Him with his hands, all serving as significant support for what he's about to proclaim about the Savior.

> **PERSONAL REFLECTION:** Out of the three sensory interactions John had with Jesus, which would mean the most to you at this place in your life. To see Him? Touch Him? Hear Him? (I realize some of these naturally overlap but don't get too technical.)

John's personal interaction with Jesus certainly affected the force and passion of his letter, but there's more to his emphatic proclamation of Jesus' physical and historical presence than what we catch on the surface. At the time of John's writing, approximately A.D. 90, the first seedlings of a heretical belief system known as gnosticism were germinating beneath the soil of the church's foundational teaching. We'll talk more about this as we go, but for now it's important to know that the gnostics (or pre-gnostics in John's time) recoiled at the idea of a Savior who took on bodily form. Since they viewed the body as inherently evil, the notion of a supreme god taking on human flesh was an inconceivable, even disgraceful, thought. This eventually led to docetism, which is the belief that Jesus only seemed to be human.[8]

Docetism: the belief that Jesus only seemed to be human.

John, on the other hand, celebrated the very thing the gnostics abhorred—the physical nature of a Savior whose face could be beheld with human eyes, whose voice could be known in a crowd, and whose breast could be leaned upon.

Read 1 John 1:3-4. According to verse 3, why did John proclaim what he'd seen and heard about Jesus?

(eternal Life) may have fellowship

Quick Review: What is docetism?

Jesus only appeared to be human

Women have often expressed to me their loneliness. Wives, single women, mothers, businesswomen all feel like outsiders or that no one really knows them. Having children or grandchildren doesn't seem to be the remedy; neither does being married, or not, because loneliness is pervasive even for the people who supposedly have it all.

I have felt desperately lonely at times, perhaps causing John's words "so that you also may have fellowship with us" to be especially meaningful. Do you hear the call of community? At the core of John's writing we find an invitation for togetherness. Perhaps you've never considered how fundamental community is to the core of the Christian faith. Studying 1 John 1:3-4 has revitalized my own understanding of this.

At the core of John's writing we find an invitation for togetherness.

PERSONAL REFLECTION: What obstacles keep you from having honest and regular fellowship? (For example: insecurities, fears, forms of busyness, bitterness that keeps you removed.)

You may have heard the Greek word for fellowship—*koinonia*. The word means *having in common,*[9] *joint ownership,* or *partnership.*[10] That John invited his readers to share in the richness of his community is beautiful, but he takes this fellowship an astounding step further.

With whom else did John invite us to share fellowship? "with the Father and with his Son, ___Jesus___ ___Christ___."

You may think John's invitation for his readers to fellowship with the Father and His Son was specific to that period of history. But read what Jesus prayed for all who would come to believe in Him in John 17:20-23.

PERSONAL TAKE: Jesus prayed that the church would be brought together in complete unity. He also prayed that we would dwell in the Father and in the Son so that the world would know God had sent Jesus. How does our fellowship with other believers and with Jesus serve as an inviting testimony to those who have yet to believe?

A good friend working through this study admitted how hard it can be for her to come out of her shell. "It took all of my being every week to come to Bible study," she said, "but after every time I felt refueled and encouraged." Sometimes it's hard for me to get out of my house for a dinner or coffee, much more a Bible study. As much as we say we long for community we often don't have it because we're afraid, have put up walls, or are holding grudges. This not only isolates our hearts, but others miss out on the uniqueness of what only we can bring.

PERSONAL RESPONSE: If you're retreating from fellowship, can you pinpoint any areas of selfishness?

When I read 1 John 1:3-4, I can sense John's passion escaping through his repeated and expressive word choices like *testify* and *proclaim,* all for the purpose of extending the hand of fellowship so that not one of his readers—not one of us—would ever have to be alone! I can almost hear his voice through his pen: You're invited. Join the community. You can be part of the team. Come be with us.

PERSONAL REFLECTION: Briefly write about a memorable time of fellowship. What did you talk about? Who specifically encouraged you? How was Christ central to the occasion?

Perhaps the most pronounced picture of fellowship I've experienced is when I'm in the Amazon region of Brazil at Justice and Mercy Amazon's Annual Jungle Pastors' Conference. I share the deepest bond with these

"I pray not only for these, but also for those who believe in Me through their message. May they all be one, as You, Father, are in Me and I am in You. May they also be one in Us, so the world may believe You sent Me. I have given them the glory You have given Me. May they be one as We are one. I am in them and You are in Me. May they be made completely one, so the world may know You have sent Me and have loved them as You have loved Me.
John 17:20-23 HCSB

pastors and their wives, which is surprising because we're from vastly different backgrounds and cultures, having virtually nothing in common but Jesus. When they tell me their stories of Jesus meeting them in hardship I cry. When they deliver a report about a child being healed my heart swells, and when I ask them for prayer they enter in on my behalf. Their spirits lift my own and my spirit theirs. We share so little in common, yet we share everything, because we share Christ.

We might expect John to say he was proclaiming his message so his readers could have salvation or eternal life or forgiveness of sins. But John offers us community! "Properly understood, this is the meaning of salvation in its widest embrace, including reconciliation to God in Christ … and incorporation in the church."[11] John gives two foundational reasons for writing. The first we've already established: so that we can have fellowship with the community of believers and with Jesus.

> What second reason does John give in verse 4?
>
> Make Joy complete

The absolute, irrevocable result of fellowship is joy. So why are so many of us dragging ourselves to church or Bible study? Why are we bored with religion? Why would we rather do anything than stand around a crusty tin of lasagna making small talk with church people?

Many factors contribute, but one is we've stopped being real with one another. Recently when I ran into a friend and asked the normal "How are you?" She gave me an honest response. She told me she'd just had a really hard conversation with her husband and how painful it was and how God was working in their marriage. Can I tell you that this was the most refreshing 25 minutes of my weekend? A fellow believer was honest with me, which helped me be honest with her. As a result I believe we had fellowship. You'd go to church for this, I promise.

We forget that the Christian life is about our fellowship with a living Person, Jesus. When He's active in our lives and in the lives of others we'll have endless things to talk, dream, and pray about. We'll have fellowship, and fellowship will lead to joy. No fleeting pleasure compares to the joy that comes from fellowship—even fellowship in the midst of suffering. When Jesus is in our midst and we're joined together with Him and with one another, the common bond of our Savior ignites heart-bursting joy. And for this joy, John is writing. Stepping back a moment, let's see how John's perspective on fellowship and its accompanying joy may have changed over the years. Take a look at Mark 9:38-41.

WHAT LOVE IS

Why did John tell the man who was driving out demons to stop?

☑ He was not one of the disciples' own.

❑ He was cursing while he cast out demons.

❑ He belonged to a different denomination.

❑ He was wearing a toupee.

PERSONAL TAKE: Reflect on John's exclusive attitude in Mark's Gospel versus his passionate invitation in 1 John 1:3. How has his perspective significantly changed?

So we might have fellowship

If our fellowship with the Lord and other believers is stale we'll tend to become judgmental, draw harsh lines, or go the opposite way and dismiss the need for fellowship altogether. But if we're communing with the Lord on a regular basis, we won't be able to help our desire to invite others into the community of believers. While I want us to be deeply grateful for our invitation into the fellowship of believers, I want us to be equally passionate about inviting others into that fellowship.

PERSONAL RESPONSE: If you are lacking joy, push outside of yourself and ask a coworker who needs you to coffee, invite someone to church who might not normally go, take a few friends and pray over someone who's sick. Write down one tangible way you can extend the hand of fellowship to someone else.

With the advent of social media and the Internet we're in danger of replacing fellowship for something that is merely a shadow of the real thing. We can download a sermon instead of sitting next to someone on a Sunday morning, we can email a prayer instead of physically enfolding another hand in our own, tweets and posts can be our manna instead of communing with God in His Word. Let's push out of our private worlds and embrace the very gift John gives us as his reason for writing: the glory of fellowship.

PERSONAL TAKE: John's physical and tangible experiences with Jesus are vital to the premise of his letter for several reasons. Based on your understanding of the first three verses, why do you think John felt it important to stress that he and the apostles had encountered Jesus so closely? Respond in the margin.

Throughout the study, I'll highlight several theological truths in the margin notated by a picture of an ingredient. Whenever you see one of these ingredients, turn to page 181 and handwrite the theological truth next to its corresponding picture. By the study's end you will have completed a list of biblical "ingredients" foundational to the Christian faith.

God is
light;
in Him
there
is no
darkness
at all
(1 John 1:5)

WALKING IN THE LIGHT

Today I'm going to encourage you to read 1 John 1:5-7 and then get your thoughts down before I start sharing any of my own. Ask the Holy Spirit to reveal Himself to you as you read, remembering that whatever the Spirit reveals to you directly through His Word will be more powerful than anything another person can offer. Also, I want you to read these verses three times through, briefly recording something different that stood out to you after each reading.

First Reading: *"if"*

Second Reading: *Message from him*

Third Reading: *God is Light.*

What new central word has emerged?

- ❑ love
- ❑ life
- ☑ light
- ❑ lord

While John doesn't explicitly say what walking in the darkness means here, he implies something: When we claim to have fellowship with God yet walk in darkness, we do not live by the ____*Truth*____.

According to John, why is it impossible to have fellowship with God while walking in darkness? Explain his logic.

we Lie
Truth not in us —

In summary, John has proclaimed the Word of life, which has been from the very beginning and has also appeared in the flesh. John proclaims to us this person, this Savior, whom he's heard, seen, and touched so that we can have fellowship with Him and with one another. And this fellowship leads to joy. But there's more—in verse 5 we discover a message Jesus taught, and John is now proclaiming. Some argue that the rest of the book hangs from this message.

What is the message? God is ____*Light*____; in Him is no ____*darkness*____.

PERSONAL TAKE: What do you love most about each side of this coin or double truth?

• God is light … *Walk in the Light*

• no darkness is in Him …

This means so much more than we can possibly cover in a day's study or even a lifetime. But one reality that really blesses me as a result of God being both light and without darkness is that He has nothing to hide. We can trust Him. "God doesn't have any dark folds in His cloak."[12] So often we're waiting for the other shoe to drop, the hammer to fall. We believe the lie that God is somehow holding out on us. If only we could crack the code we'd finally be accepted and gain His blessing. But we're not dealing with a duplicitous God on the run. We're dealing with Light. He's revealed Himself. Laid Himself bare in the open and in a light so clean and bright only His holiness could withstand it. And He's not just in the light, He is the light.

Re-read verses 6-7. According to those verses …

What is impossible? *to have fellowship c̄ him & walk in darkness –*

What is possible? *walk in the light – fellowship c̄ one another.*

The fixed rule of God being light serves as the basis for John's argument: A person can't have fellowship with a God who is light while walking in darkness. The way John writes sometimes reminds me of those dreaded word problems from Algebra class: If a bus leaves New York at 6:32 a.m. and is traveling at 53 MPH, and a train leaves Chicago at 9:51 a.m. and is traveling at 91 MPH, how many people on the bus from New York are wearing hats? (At least this is how I remember these things going.)

John's reasoning is a little more straightforward: If God is light and there is no darkness in light, you can't say you have fellowship with God while living in darkness. It's a pretty simple formula. A simple formula I have complicated and clouded over the years in an attempt to justify my choices and behavior that were contrary to God's light. It's amazing how easy it is to reason away something so plain. One of my friends brilliantly put it this way, "For a time I really wanted to live in the dark so I tried to make the dark work for me."

Note: John opens this section with "This is the message we have heard from Him [Jesus]." The word *message* in the Greek is *angelia* and is only used two times in the New Testament, once here and the other in 1 John 3:11. The message is what John and the apostles had received directly from Jesus and he passes that message on, beginning with the statement that God is light. Interestingly, there is no quote of Jesus' in the Gospels where He says that God is light in exactly those terms.

PERSONAL REFLECTION: Briefly describe a situation where you tried to make living in the darkness "work for you." Did you simultaneously try to convince yourself you were staying close to God? What were the results?

Light is a prominent concept in both the Old and New Testaments, a visible reality written about and also a metaphor used to describe a spiritual reality. One of my favorite ways to better understand the biblical meaning of a word is to look at its usages in other places in Scripture.

Read the following Old Testament passages and answer the corresponding questions, keeping today's text in mind.

Genesis 1:3-4: What did God separate from the light, and how might this separation relate to John's statement in verse 6?

darkness -

Exodus 13:20-22: What did God's gift of fire allow the Israelites to do beyond being able to see?

travel by night

2 Samuel 22:29: What does David call the Lord in his prayer and why?

My Lamp
turning darkness into light

The passages in Exodus and Samuel remind me of a wonderful insight by the late beloved pastor John Stott, "The effect of the light is not just to make people see, but to enable them to walk."[13] I love being able to move in life, both physically and spiritually. But how often I've relied on my legs to carry me and my eyes to lead me, all the while taking for granted the light that allows me to know where I'm going in the first place.

PERSONAL REFLECTION: Can you think of a time when choosing a path of darkness literally obscured your ability to see where you were going in life?

When you read verse 6, one of two things may have happened: 1) A sin you've struggled with or are currently struggling with may have come to mind. The result may be a sinking sensation leaving you wondering if you really love God or if you're just another deceived casualty who can't actually live life by the truth. Or, 2) you may have immediately thought of someone who claims to love God but who's materialistic, in an immoral relationship, drinks too much, doesn't believe Jesus is the only way to salvation, watches trashy television, or fill in your blank.

Let's address these in order. Without softening what John is saying in these verses, we need to remember the false teaching that had crept into the church at the time. We will continue to gather from John's writings and historical references that certain people who were claiming to have fellowship with God were living in a way contrary to their claim. For the protection of the believers, John clearly addressed this by stating that if someone was claiming to have fellowship (be in partnership, participate) with God, then his or her life would naturally demonstrate that. So while the statement is a truth for all of us, part of John's reason for writing was to alert the believers about these false teachers.

In addition, note John's use of the words *walking in darkness*. This can be translated as *living habitually in darkness*. The phrase "implies determination to choose sin (darkness) rather than God (light) as one's constant sphere of existence."[14] So, if after reading verse 6, you are burdened by a certain sin, something that is affecting your fellowship and communion with God, this is conviction. Conviction is the Holy Spirit working in you and should be heeded. He ultimately leads you to confession and repentance. But experiencing conviction is different than having no remorse or concern for your behavior, claiming to know God while living contrary to His nature. The people John is writing about were walking, living in, and even enjoying, the darkness.

On the flip side, if your mind immediately raced to someone who claims to love God but who seems to be living in opposition to His Word and nature I will ask you a few questions I always have to ask myself. (Keep in mind it's easy to get bent out of shape by someone else's walking in darkness while we are doing the same thing in another area.)

1. How would you best describe your heart toward this person? Strike a dash along the line.

|---|

self-righteous and judgmental   genuinely aching and concerned

2. Do you care more about being right than about the person you're concerned for? Are you trying to guard your stance on an issue, hang on to control of a relationship, safeguard your position? Or, are you truly motivated by a heart that longs to see this person free of sin, walking in the light? Write your thoughts in the margin.

3. Are you close enough to the person to gently and lovingly talk to him or her (see Gal. 6:1)? If so, would you pray about doing so?

PERSONAL RESPONSE OPTION 1: If you find yourself convicted over sins you're practicing in the darkness—secret sins you have to cover up from people who are "walking in the light," would you take time to write a prayer of confession to the Lord while also taking steps to walk in freedom and light? This may be the most important moment for you in this study.

PERSONAL RESPONSE OPTION 2: If you have a friend or acquaintance who claims to love God but who's living a habitual life in the darkness, write out a prayer for him or her, not mentioning any specific names.

I can't let you go without another look at the benefits of verse 7. What two gifts of grace come with walking in the light?

The blood
of Jesus purifies
us from all sin
(1 John 1:7)

Have you ever felt guilt so heavy it threatened to sink you, shame so attached to your being you thought you could never be rid of its disgrace? Maybe you live with a regret that never ceases haunting you. If so, I'm not sure if a more beautiful, more relieving word could greet us than the word *cleanse* or *purify*. Our total cleansing is only possible because of the blood of Jesus given for us at the cross. Reflect on this gift. As you ponder what this means in your life, let me leave you once again with John Stott's insightful words, "The verb [purifies] suggests that God does more than forgive; he erases the stain of sin."[15] Could a more glorious truth lead us today, tomorrow, and forevermore?

THE THINGS WE SAY

My brother, his wife and two young children have moved to Nashville—please insert all the aunt excitement you can possibly imagine. They arrived during the fortunate months of football season where I can be readily found in the kitchen stirring soups and chilis, happily refilling endless bowls of chips and salsa that could keep Mexico hopping for decades.

Having 3-year-old Will scamper around the living room with both arms barely reaching around his football, pleading "tackle me, tackle me," is an anchor I had no idea I was missing. And then there was the evening he arrived with his new doctor's kit full of all manner of plastic tools, doling out shots and listening intently for pulses. At one point when I went to tackle him—because this had been such a fun activity two days earlier—Will halted me with his hand. "No, don't tackle me," he said, "I'm a doctor!" Oh, the beauty of being three. You can wake up a soldier, a firefighter, a chef, a drummer, whatever suits your fancy. This works well when you're a toddler but is not as effective when you're twenty-four and applying for a job.

Still, as much as we may grow out of certain ways of thinking, I think we all wish to some degree we could snap our fingers and simply decide what we want to be true, or not true, about ourselves. According to today's reading, believing whatever you want to believe about yourself was an issue during the John's day as well. Like today, it led to all sorts of wrong conclusions. People were claiming certain ideas about their natures, while John was pointing to the immutable truths about us. We'll see how this is still happening today.

> Conviction is the Holy Spirit working in you and should be heeded.

Read 1 John 1:5-10 (including re-reading your text from yesterday). John uses the statement "If we say" (or "If we claim") three times in these verses. Fill in the statements below:

Verse 6: If we say/claim _to have fellowship_

yet we _Walk in darkness_

we _Lie + do not live by the truth —_

Verse 8: If we say/claim _To be without sin_

we _deceve ourselfs_

and the _truth is not in us –_

Verse 10: If we say/claim _we have not Sinned_

we make _him out to be a Liar_

and _his word has no place in our Lives_

PERSONAL TAKE: How would you describe the difference between being without sin and not sinning? The difference is subtle but do your best.

Choose one of the aforementioned mentalities and write about how we see this belief cropping up in current culture.

Recently a friend was explaining his belief system to me, a worldview that does not include the idea of sin. When I asked him how he accounted for the horrible things that go on in the world, such as murder, abuse, theft, child abandonment, he said that these were a result of ignorance; we don't do bad things because we're sinners but because we're ignorant of God's love. He continued to explain that as we go on in life (even in future lives) our ignorance will eventually mature into enlightenment and we won't want to do these things anymore.

My friend's perspective may represent an extreme end of the spectrum, but whether we are talking about being people who don't sin (closely related: we minimize sin), or inherently being without sin (closely related: we're basically innocent), these ideas are widely adopted. All we have to do is tune into anything pop culture to see people justifying sin or flat-out denying its existence. Because we're so indoctrinated with culture's viewpoint of sin— myself included—let's get specific here so we can see where we may be being deceived.

An example of claiming to be without sin altogether might look like this: "I did some things in my life that maybe weren't the smartest, but we're all basically innocent. I've always tried to love people and my heart is good." This would be to deny the biblical reality of original sin, that we are born into a stream of humanity that is fallen and sinful. (And still very much loved, but this comes in a moment.) While not popular in modern culture, it is biblical to own the sinfulness of our human hearts apart from Jesus.

An example of claiming to not sin might look like this: "I don't feel bad about having an affair on my husband because I'm not in love with him anymore." This is a situation where a person recognizes that sin exists, but explains away her specific sin. She justifies it, rationalizes it, buys a self-help book that excuses it, or sweeps it under the rug.

When I taught through the book of 1 John in my home, one of my dear friends would occasionally cross her eyes and tilt her head back while I was teaching. It was her way of telling me that she was starting to get lost in all the John-isms of "if-this… then-that" and that I should insert a funny story if I wanted one single soul to return the following week. I will admit that John's writings are dense and sometimes difficult to assimilate. So if you're in any way trying to make sense of the three claims, how about the simplicity of one scholar's insight: All three of these claims "are really variations on a single theme: 'sin does not affect me.'"[16] There it is. Sin does not affect me. It's the crux of the three claims and a thousand more. This mentality is what has broken God's heart, destroyed relationships, and wounded our own souls.

> **PERSONAL REFLECTION:** Ask the Lord to show you any sin in your life that you believe doesn't affect you. We desperately need Him to shine a light on these areas. Our very communion with God and with others is at stake.

Now let's look at the effects of believing the three claims you've already listed. I've filled in some for you.

Verse 6: We lie and _do not live by truth_

Verse 8: We _deceive ourselves_ and the truth is not in us

Verse 10: We make God a liar and His _Word_ is not in us.

John's words are strong, but we have to keep in mind the context in which he was writing. The ideas of false teachers had infiltrated the purity of the Gospel John and the other apostles preached. At a minimum three false claims were floating around: 1) some said they knew God but walked in ways contrary to God's nature, 2) some said they were without sin, and 3) some recognized sin in the world but believed they had not sinned.

PERSONAL REFLECTION: Of the three claims in the margin, which is most difficult for you to handle in society? Why?

The most difficult one for me is the claim to love God while disregarding what the whole of Scripture says about a certain matter or behavior. I know, these are not the three topics of discussion you're anxious to bring up at your next dinner party—I actually tried it recently. But as we move toward the more hopeful side of these verses, keep John's heart in mind. Don't forget his passion. Or even his age. John was at the end of his years, he'd lived a lot of life, seen the death of Jesus, touched Him after His resurrection, taken Jesus' mother into his home, pastored the first generation of believers. At this point, and with so much at stake, John's not about to get fuzzy or soft on his readers. But here's the treasure: As emphatically as John talks about the dangers of walking in darkness or denying sin, he equally proclaims the gifts and graces of walking in the light. If 1 John had a list of celebrity verses, verse 9 would be one of them:

"If we confess our sins, he is __faithful__ and __just__ and will forgive us our sins and to cleanse us from all unrighteousness."

PERSONAL TAKE: Why do you think John used these particular two words in relation to God's forgiveness toward us?

When we confess our sins, He is faithful and just to forgive us our sins and purify us from all unrighteousness (1 John 1:9)

The confession John is talking about is not only agreeing with God that we have sinned, but also expressing a desire to turn away from that sin, to make a plan not to return to it. This doesn't mean we'll never sin again—John will address this shortly—but our heart's attitude should not look for a bit of forgiveness just to vindicate us so we can get back to the sin we were enjoying before we confessed it.

> Proverbs 28:13 gives us a good picture of this. What additional action is mentioned? Confession and…
>
> ❑ fasting   ✓ renouncing
> ❑ forgetting   ❑ feeling really, really bad

Now I want to circle back to John's use of the words *faithful* and *righteous* (some translations say *just*) in relation to His forgiving us. Earlier I asked you to comment on why you think John used these two words. I'd love to know your thoughts because they're not necessarily words you'd put together. When I think of what it feels like to have sinned, coming before someone who is faithful is a comforting thought, but standing before someone who's looking to mete out justice can be a terrifying idea.

With so much at stake, John's not about to get fuzzy or soft on his readers.

When we sin, we don't really want justice because "Justice is associated in our minds with punishment or acquittal, not with forgiveness."[17] But herein lies the beautiful gift of Christ. Though God does require that justice be served for our sins, Christ's death and resurrection has satisfied those requirements. Because of Jesus, God can remain faithful to His covenant toward us, offering forgiveness toward those who seek Him.

PERSONAL RESPONSE: When it comes to forgiveness of sins, which word—*faithful*, or *righteous*—means the most to you and why?

Here's the best part—we can walk in the light. In the light with God and in the light with others. No more hiding, covering up, shirking, or manipulating. We receive a new quality of life and its most impressive characteristic is that it's a life lived in the light.

We've looked at some dense material this week, but my prayer is that, together, we're closing the week more hopeful. The more time I spend with John, the more he reminds me of an elderly grandfather who's seen enough of life to have little use for a filter; he tells it like it is. In a world of howling opinions and shifting sands, I'm grateful and relieved we can exhale at the unshakable thought of clinging to "That which we have heard from the beginning." The Word of Life.

NONNA'S MEAT SAUCE

FROM THE KITCHEN OF NONNA

You'll love this pasta sauce recipe for its flavor. I think the ground fennel seed and pancetta are what make the noticeable difference, but you don't have to actually tell people this. Again, just resort to the phrase, this old recipe? It was nothing. Really. Serve with warm bread and a crisp salad.

INGREDIENTS

- 2 tablespoons extra virgin olive oil
- 3 tablespoons butter
- 1 medium yellow or white onion, finely chopped *(about 1 cup)*
- 4 cloves of garlic
- 2 stalks celery, finely chopped *(about 3/4 cup)*
- 1 small carrot, peeled and finely chopped *(about 1/2 cup)*
- 1 tablespoon freshly ground fennel seed *(I like to grind my own seeds for an extra fresh flavor)*
- 1/2 pound ground beef *(or veal)*
- 1/2 pound ground pork
- 2 ounces pancetta, finely chopped
- Salt and pepper, to taste
- 1/2 cup dry white wine, good quality
- 2 *(15 ounce)* cans of plum tomatoes with juice
- 3 tablespoons orange juice

DIRECTIONS:

1. Heat a large sauce pan or Dutch oven over medium heat.

2. Add the oil and two tablespoons of butter until melted.

3. Add the onion, garlic, celery, and carrot and lightly sauté, stirring occasionally, until the vegetables are soft, but not brown, about 15 minutes.

4. Add the fennel seed and cook until fragrant, about 1 to 2 minutes.

5. Add the ground beef, pork, and pancetta and a pinch of salt. Break up the meat while cooking, until the meat is no longer pink, but not overdone, about 10 minutes.

6. Add the wine and simmer until it has reduced completely.

7. Add the tomatoes and their juices, along with the orange juice, reduce the heat to very low and barely simmer, stirring occasionally, about 30 minutes.

8. Right before serving, and after you've taken the sauce off the burner, add the remaining tablespoon of butter and allow to melt into the sauce.

9. Season to taste with salt and pepper. Serve over rigatoni, or your favorite pasta.

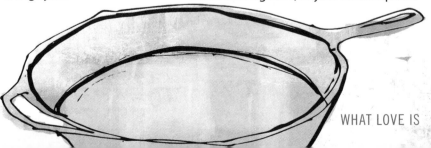

STRAWBERRY ROMAINE SALAD

FROM THE KITCHEN OF MY MOM

DRESSING

- 1 cup oil
- 1/2 cup red wine vinegar
- 1/4-1/2 cup sugar to your preference
- 2 minced cloves garlic
- 1/2 tsp salt
- 1/2 tsp paprika (don't leave this out)
- 1/4 tsp white pepper
- Mix in blender and chill

SALAD:

- 1 large head romaine, chopped.
- 1 head of Boston lettuce or another similar type.
- I pint of sliced strawberries
- 1 cup finely shredded Monterey Jack cheese
- 1/2 cup toasted chopped walnuts
- Toss salad in dressing and serve.

If you want to mix up the flavor a bit, you can use a little sesame oil, add chopped water chestnuts for crunch, and/or add in some fresh ginger.

LIVING FOR WHAT LASTS

I can't wait for you to immerse yourself in this week's passages from chapters 2 and 3 of 1 John. They hold some of the most significant truths and treasures of our faith, all the way from the Advocate we have in Christ, to the closeness between light and love, to living as overcomers. I want the knowledge of these realities to permeate my being because they change our everydays. This week's verses include one of 1 John's most well known imperatives about not loving the things of the world because "the world and its desires pass away." We'll look at this in greater depth but it's this piece about the fleeting nature of the world system and the fickleness of it all that I once held in my hand in the form of a rubber seed.

I was somewhere on the Amazon River puttering through the jungle in a small boat. A few of us were scouting for wildlife in the trees—wide-eyed and glued to the foliage like fourth graders on a field trip. We were moving at an unremarkable pace when suddenly our driver Gennison downshifted and slid the steering wheel slightly toward the right bank with intent. He'd seen something. Maybe an anaconda coiled in a tree; a spider monkey swinging by his tail; a row of toucans harmonizing on a branch; a sloth doing absolutely nothing. Imagine my disappointment when Gennison plucked a shell from a tree, cracked it open and handed me a rubber seed. I almost fell into the water from boredom. It was about the size of an oblong golf ball, smoother than a sanded piece of wood and variegated with light and dark browns. I tried to act excited the way you did when you were a child at a friend's house for dinner and the mom made you try asparagus for the first time. In light of hoping to find exotic wildlife, the rubber seed was, scientifically speaking, *womp, womp*. That is, if you don't understand the significance of the rubber seed to the city of Manaus.

Manaus is an interesting city in that it at one time was envisioned to be the jewel of the Amazon. Whenever I visit, though, I'm faced with the sad reality that it hasn't yet reached its potential. In many ways Manaus is the attractive boyfriend brimming with wit and personality but with a few setbacks: poverty, crime, drugs, and alcohol abuse abound, despite the stunning views of the river and natural resources of the jungle. Driving down the streets you would never know that "Manaus had electricity before London, telephones before Rio de Janeiro, and electric trams when New Yorkers were still staring at horses' backsides."[1] The rubber seed had made this possible.

During the late 19th century Manaus played center stage to a rubber boom that ushered in wealth as generously flowing as the river. The rubber tree plantations in Amazonas were exploding, offering superior rubber to the exports of Africa and Central America. Between 1898 and 1910 the party was in full swing as rubber accounted for twenty-six percent of Brazil's export revenue, supporting the big hit of bicycles and automobiles in Europe and The United States. Money was literally growing on trees and the plantation owners were spending it like the water they lived on. The industry tycoons were dreaming up ways to enjoy their wealth. My Brazilian friend Francie loves to remind us of this while walking through Manaus' downtown plaza. She tells the story of how the rubber-rich would ship their clothes to be cleaned in Europe, because why not spend money on that? And this was just the beginning. No act was too extravagant for the rubber barons capitalizing on the exploding industry. Some even quenched their horses' thirst with champagne.

In 1910 the British and the Dutch pulled the plug on the party, having figured out how to establish rubber tree plantations using cheap labor on concentrated plots of land in Asia. Others blame Sir Henry Wickham, an English explorer who claimed to have smuggled rubber tree seeds out of the Amazonas. Supposedly he went on to cultivate them in England's Kew Gardens and later the Brits transported them to their respective Asian colonies. While Brazilians were forced to extract latex deep in the Amazon forest, the plantations in Asia were cultivated in easily accessible territories, yielding high quality rubber at a low price point. Whether or not Sir Henry extracted those seeds out of their indigenous habitat, or they simply existed halfway around the world, in 1910 the bubble burst and the ephemeral heyday Manaus was enjoying came to an abrupt end. "'The Golden City' with too much money" couldn't last at this rate.[2] Why? Because the stuff of this world never does.

Holding that rubber seed in my hand could have represented a thousand pursuits we put our trust in or hang our hopes on. I used to look at John's warning about not loving the world, or anything in the world, from a mostly negative standpoint. Ugh, I thought. I knew we weren't supposed to love sin, but John just went ahead and put the whole world off-limits. (Not exactly, we'll see.) But what I'd somehow missed was his double caveat: The world is temporal; the will of God is eternal. Things like fame and bonuses, new cars and second homes, stock options and rubber booms, even good health and prized relationships, or anything we live for that isn't motivated by a love for God and His will, will prove temporary. But whatever we do while abiding in Christ—a distinctly Johannine theme—will last forever. In other words, there's a really positive reason for why John steers us away from a love of momentary pleasures to the real, eternal stuff.

If we're going to hold a seed in our hand, John wants it to be one that will bear much fruit, fruit that will last.

VIEWER GUIDE

FELLOWSHIP

GROUP DISCUSSION QUESTIONS:

What was the most impacting moment for you this week? It may be a Bible verse, principle, prayer experience, revelation, new understanding, or conviction.

How can you be more intentional about giving yourself to Christian fellowship? What keeps you from fellowship (fear, past wounds, insecurity, busyness, selfishness)?

Did you learn anything new about John's earlier life as a young disciple that surprised you? (Week 1, Day 1)

What about Jesus being the Word of Life gives you hope in trying circumstances? (p. 17)

Describe a time when you minimized or justified sin in your life. How did this attitude diminish your gratitude for Christ forgiving your sins and cleansing you from all unrighteousness? (See 1 John 1:9, p. 34.)

AN ADVOCATE

I visited a local Bible study the other night. They'd just finished studying the book of Ruth and they had cupcakes on hand, so it was a stellar night. One of the women in the group asked if I find myself circling back to portions of Scripture I'm writing about. Do I sit down to study briefly and eventually realize the Lord has this whole picnic planned for an extended weekend, or year's worth of work connected to a certain text? The answer to her question was yes, and today's verses may be two of those. As I've studied and pondered them I realize the message is far deeper, more personal and freeing than what we can possibly fit into a day's analysis. So I encourage you to linger with the Lord today, and if today is not a lingering kind of day because you have a paper due or your kids have runny noses or you're prepping for a presentation, go ahead and work through today's study as normal, but later plot out some time, somewhere, to drink deeply of the fountain John leads us to today.

Read 1 John 2:1-2. In what endearing way does John address the reader? My _dear_ _Children_.

We'll see this affectionate address used several times in John's letters. His deep filial love for his readers is a thread we can't let go of, especially when John's words become more forceful or black and white. No matter how strong he sometimes comes across we can always fall back into the loving hands with which he writes—we are his dear children.

What specific reason does he give for writing at the top of verse 1?
heard, eyes, hands - We proclaim.

When John says, "I am writing this, so that..." he is referring to what he's already written, as opposed to what he's about to write. In other words, all the points he's already made about light versus darkness, forgiveness in Jesus, fellowship with God and other believers, etc. are meant to be the basis for why we shouldn't sin. Instead of saying "don't sin because I said so," I appreciate that John gives us a little more to go on, actually a full chapter's worth. He takes "not sinning" out of the realm of legalism and mindlessly trying to keep the rules for the rules' sake, and speaks to us like a father to his children.

PERSONAL TAKE: Look back over chapter 1. Out of the compelling truths John writes about, which one most compels you not to sin? I'll give you my response to get you thinking: I don't want to live in the darkness, because it requires living in secret, covering up, missing out on the peace that accompanies walking in the light.

As much as I love the first part of verse one about not sinning, I'm thankful for John's provision through verse two. For consistency I'm including the HCSB version below:

"My little children, I am writing you these things so that you may not sin. But if anyone does sin, we have an advocate with the Father—Jesus Christ the Righteous One. (2) He Himself is the propitiation for our sins, and not only for ours, but also for those of the whole world."

Let's first break down the three different ways John refers to Jesus in these verses:

1. We have an ___*Advocate*___ with the Father (NIV 84 says "one who speaks to the Father in our defense.")

2. He is Jesus Christ, the …
☐ Savior ☐ Redeemer ☐ Healer ☑ Righteous One

3. He Himself is the *atoning Sacrifice* for our sins.

ADVOCATE

PERSONAL REFLECTION: Let's start with this comforting word *Advocate*. Briefly describe a time when you had an advocate come to your aid. What did he or she do on your behalf and how did you feel in response? What characteristics defined this person? (Don't skip this reflection because I want you to get in touch with what having an advocate meant to you.)

Jesus Christ is our Advocate before the Father (1 John 2:1)

The word *advocate* in John's writing is the Greek word *parakletos*. It means *one called alongside to help, counsel, or protect*. The noun *parakletos* occurs only in Johannine literature, typically used to describe the Holy Spirit, making this mention of Christ especially compelling.

John's writings are referred to as Johannine literature.

> Based on 1 John 2:1, at what very specific time in our lives do we need Christ as our Advocate?
>
> *When we sin —*

You may not need help personalizing the idea of Christ as your Advocate, but perhaps you can think of a time when guilt overwhelmed you, when you were grieved by what you were capable of, shocked by the depth of sin that enslaved you. Then you discovered that Jesus is not only your Savior-for-heaven, but your Advocate-right-now. He speaks on your behalf before God in the heavenlies. What you just discovered in the first verse of chapter 2 is that Jesus, our Advocate, meets us—not at our point of achievement—but at our point of failure![3] I will go out on a limb and say that in all of life no truth is more freeing than Jesus as our Advocate. Oh for grace to understand it even more than I do.

Jesus, our Advocate, meets us—not at our point of achievement—but at our point of failure!

RIGHTEOUS ONE

> You already noted that John specified our Advocate as Jesus Christ, the Righteous One. Why do you think it was important for John to mention Jesus as righteous in this context?

I remember receiving a letter informing me my new health insurance was only going to be partial coverage. I went through all the normal channels and couldn't get anyone to budge. I tried excessive kindness, pretended to be no-nonsense, phoned several different representatives, threatened to leave them (as if my monthly premium mattered to their trillion dollar business). I was sure someone would eventually help me, except I kept getting funneled back to poor Anita who was so done with me.

After a week of this, a friend put me in touch with a man she knew who was a lawyer for my insurance company. He said he'd be glad to help me, and after one phone call I received a magic letter from the company saying "Congratulations! You have full coverage! You are the best client we've ever had!," or something like that. I share this story, not because this is how most of my life goes, but because of how it felt to have an advocate in a situation where I was totally powerless.

Typically we need an advocate who holds a position we don't, has power we don't possess, is granted access to people we can't get to, has influence we're without. This is why John's reference to Jesus as the Righteous Advocate is so critical! As sinners, laid bare before a holy God, we need Someone who has what we don't—righteousness.

When standing as sinners before a holy God we need Someone who has what we don't—righteousness.

According to Hebrews 4:13-16, why are we able to approach the throne of grace with confidence? *c̄ Christ -*

How is Jesus' function in Hebrews as our High Priest similar to His function of Advocate in 1 John 2:1-2? *Atonement -*

PERSONAL RESPONSE: Perhaps you're currently fostering sin in your life—secret or otherwise—and you're desperate for rescue. You need Jesus who has the righteousness you don't have, the access you need to the Father, the mercy to intercede on your behalf. Write a prayer of confession to your Advocate. He promises to forgive and purify you (see 1 John 1:9). Respond in the margin.

PROPITIATION

I know this has already been somewhat of a full day, so maybe this is not the best time to toss out a word like *propitiation.* Just know that I'm aware. The term means *the removal of divine wrath.* More fully, "Jesus' death is the means that turns God's wrath from the sinner."[4]

Removal of guilt.

PERSONAL TAKE: Notice that John says that Jesus is the propitiation for our sins. How is this more personal and costly than if John had written that Jesus had simply provided propitiation?

Look ahead to 1 John 4:10. What is the sole source and grounding of God's sending Jesus to be our propitiation?
❏ mercy   ❏ grace   ❏ holiness   ☑ love

Jesus Christ took God's wrath for us (1 John 2:2)

God's wrath is a difficult concept to digest, especially in our twenty-first century American mindset of "all we need is love" and "live and let live." Still, the concept is a biblical one, even if it's troubled believers and unbelievers alike over the centuries. But what may be troubling about God's wrath should make His love for us even more astounding: He sent His Son so His wrath could be turned away from us. Jesus is the propitiation for our sin. Amazing.

Choose one closing Personal Response, and answer in the margin.

PERSONAL RESPONSE 1: If you've never experienced Jesus as your Advocate, dialogue with Him about this. Ask Him to reveal Himself to you personally as your Advocate, in particular as it relates to past sin or sin you're currently dealing with.

PERSONAL RESPONSE 2: Write a prayer of thanksgiving for a specific instance in which Jesus was your Advocate, or for Him being your propitiation.

You have hung in there with a weighty day of study. Great work. Let me close by saying that we can look at the original language and dissect words like *advocate* and *propitiation,* and we can look at illustrations that help us better grasp what John's saying. But ultimately, verses 2:1-2 are best understood when experienced. I don't know where you are in your journey with the Lord, but I encourage you to pray what I'm praying for myself: that God will open our eyes to what these verses look like in our personal lives. Because if John was writing for anything, he was writing for life.

DAY 2
WE KNOW THAT WE KNOW

I remember as a child asking the Lord to save me no less than one hundred times. I even drove stakes in the backyard to remind me when the doubts came—about every other night—that I really was a Christian. As I grew older, I wondered not only if God could forgive me, but if I was forgivable at my core. Conversely, I've felt so certain of the Lord's presence, so convinced of His love that it felt impossible to ever again doubt my relationship with Him. Many of us can identify with having experienced deeply emotional communion with the Lord as well as stretches of time in His Word that felt drier than a Triscuit.

So John enters into all our emotional highs and despairing lows and offers us the word *know* 25 times in his first letter alone.[5] He wants us to not only know, but to know that we know Him. Assurance is one of John's most prevalent themes. I hope you find his words today encouraging, and that you'll think about those stakes in the backyard differently.

Throughout today's study remember that John writes so we can know that we know Jesus—not so we can doubt that we know Jesus.

Read 1 John 2:3-6, and let's lay these concepts out as plainly as possible.

Verse 3: As a characteristic of knowing God, we will naturally obey His ___*Commands*___

Verse 5: God's love is truly made complete (or perfected) in the person who obeys His ___*Word*___.

It's difficult to know here if "God's love" means His love for us, or our love for Him. I personally lean toward our love for God, since His love for us cannot be improved upon.

Verse 6: Whoever claims to live in Christ must:
- ❑ keep the Ten Commandments perfectly
- ☑ walk as Jesus did
- ❑ pray without ceasing
- ❑ put others above herself

Let's look at how closely John's words tie into the words of Jesus in John's Gospel. Read John 14:15,21,23 and 15:10.

In one sentence, sum up the theme of these verses.

God Loves Us –

Keeping God's commands is not a condition for our salvation but a characteristic of it.[6] For instance, when we see a child who looks just like her mother we know the shared resemblance isn't what caused the two of them to be related, rather their common features are the outcropping of their relatedness. In the same way, when we really know Jesus, our lives will be characterized by following Him and keeping His commands. Partly because the climate of gnosticism, which claimed a special *gnosis* or *knowledge of God*, was sweeping through the Johannine community, John was helping his people distinguish between those who really knew Jesus versus people who merely claimed to know Him. In essence, our love for Jesus will have a bearing on the way we live our lives.

PERSONAL REFLECTION: It's easy to have a bumper sticker love for Jesus, a sentiment you slap on when convenient. But it's another thing altogether to live your life seeking to obey His will laid out for us in Scripture. What is one significant action you've taken recently to obey the Lord? According to 1 John 2:3, how does this affirm your knowing Him?

Obedience

> Keeping God's commands is not a condition for our salvation but a characteristic of it.

You may be wondering what commandments John is talking about here. The Ten Commandments? Every commandment listed in the Bible? The Law? To further complicate things, he speaks of obeying both God's commands (v. 3) and His Word (v. 5).

We have our hands full with the things we do know: sexual purity, words of encouragement instead of gossip, humility in place of pride, contentment for jealousy, speaking truth instead of lying to one another.

> John inserts a strong statement in verse 4. What is it?
>
> *disobedience lea makes a Liar + truth not in him*
>
> How would you describe the difference between an imperfect believer who seeks to be obedient and a rebellious unbeliever who disregards God's commands? Respond in the margin.

Occasionally I find myself wanting to soften John, to explain to him the type of people who live in my neighborhood—people concerned with diplomacy and political correctness, who name the chickens they raise in their backyards. That said, I don't think diplomacy was high on John's list of concerns. His desire was to protect his "dear children" in the faith and to preserve the integrity of Jesus' message.

> Remember in our first week we touched on gnosticism, which was in its earliest pre-stages at the time of John's writings. From memory, what does the term *gnostic* mean? (Or look back to page 22.)

denied Jesus taking on human form –

Though many forms exist, gnosticism's basic premise is twofold: 1. The material world and the body are evil. 2. The way to be released from the imprisonment of this world and the body is through *gnosis*, or knowledge. In other words, gnostics believed that salvation is achieved through enlightenment.[7] As a result, "gnosticism in any form is seldom concerned with moral behavior; redemption for the gnostic involves a release from ignorance, not sin."[8] The gnostics didn't believe their moral behavior had any bearing on their relationship with God.[9] So you can imagine how passionate John was to assert that our love for God and our moral behavior go hand in hand. You can't have one without the other.

Understanding this climate of belief helps us better understand John's strong language and his black and white statements. He wanted to clearly carve out the difference between those who truly know God and those who merely claim to. (You can't say you know God and disregard His ways.) But while John lays out a strong caution in verse 4, he also gives us much assurance. Look back at verses 3, 5 and 6, and draw a line between the corresponding truths and characteristics below.

Truths: Characteristics

God's love is made complete in us   We obey His commands
We know that we've come to know Him   We obey His word
We know we are in Him   We walk like Jesus

Have you noticed the one thing noticeably absent from the list of how we can know that we know God? Our FEELINGS! John surprises us here, because how much do we love our feelings? We can spend days dissecting them, fueling them over a meal with friends. We even have our favorite bad feelings. The problem is that while our feelings are gifts from God they do not make the list of things to go on when it comes to having assurance about your relationship with Him.

John instead points to the less fluctuating, more stable characteristics of obedience to God's ways and living the way Jesus did. While we won't follow God perfectly (John has already said we're with sin), we should be able to look back over the course of our faith and see the direction of our lives pointing toward obedience, toward Jesus—even if the line is at points zigzagged. Could anyone say it better than the late Elizabeth Prentiss of *Stepping Heavenward*?

> *"You cannot prove to yourself that you love God by examining your feelings toward Him. They are indefinite and they fluctuate. But just as far as you obey Him, just so far, depend upon it; you love Him."*[10]

Just for review, what are three "characteristics" of a believer according to verses 3, 5 and 6? (Try to pull these from memory.)

Obeys God's __*Commands*__

Obeys God's __*Word*__

Walks as __*Jesus*__ walked.

PERSONAL RESPONSE: Since our love for the Lord and following His ways are inextricably linked, close today by spending whatever remaining time you have slowly pondering Psalm 119:33-40. These verses are a prayer specifically about a deeper understanding of the Lord's Word. I encourage you to pray these verses out loud. After you've taken thoughtful time, write in the margin the one verse that resonates with you the most.

AN OLD, NEW COMMAND

My sister Katie and I walked into an antique store south of Nashville and there, gleaming in the sun's rays dashing through the windows, was the one.

I'd been looking for a dining room table for a while, not a brand new department store table but not something that looked like it had been left on the side of the road either. Around one of its legs hung a tag that noted the table was 250 years old and had come from a church in Vermont, at which point I was trying to hoist it out of the store on my back. Someone could have totally made this information up for suckers like me. The whole church antique spiel is exactly the kind of thing that woos my heart and caused me to spend far more on an old table—with its divots, scratches, and countless imperfections—than I would have plunked down on a sparkly new one. So now I have a new, old table. You'll soon see where I'm headed with this.

Read 1 John 2:7-8 in the italics below. (Since today's text is complex I'm going with this version for consistency.)

> *"Beloved, I am not writing to you about a new law, but about an old one, which has been yours from the beginning. This old law is the message that you have heard. (8) On the other hand, I am writing to you about a new law—and this is realized in him and also in you—because the darkness is fading, and the real light is already shining."*[11]

Note that John addresses his readers as "dear friends" or "beloved" again. Let those inviting and comforting words sink in today. I know, you're rushed and you have things to do, but stop: You are beloved.

Without thinking too hard, what part of these verses stuck out to you the most and why?

darkness is fading ...

The commandment John is presenting is both old and new—sort of like my new dining room table that's 200 years old, except way more complex than this. Am I helping yet? Before really studying this book I would get to the whole old-command-new command situation and

I would think *I have no idea what this means.* So before we get too far into what's old and what's new about this command, it may help to get a handle on what the command is in the first place. Thankfully, the Gospel of John sheds light on this for us.

> What is the "new" command Jesus gave His disciples in John 13:34?
>
> *Love one another*
>
> Look back at two Old Testament passages to better understand the "old" love commands. Paraphrase the core message of each.
>
> Deuteronomy 6:4-5
>
> *heart, soul, strength ... Love*
>
> Leviticus 19:18
>
> *Love your neighbor as yourself*
>
> Now revisit John 13:34. What new element does Jesus add to the old command to love one another? "As _*I*_ have _*Loved*_ you, so you are to love one another."

After referencing this verse I remember my friend Marcie saying, "This is what makes the old commandment new—we're to love like Jesus loved. It's a whole new ball game, baby." I have at times tried to tame this verse. Don't tame it; let it push you beyond what you may think is reasonable.

> **PERSONAL REFLECTION:** Think of one prominent relationship in your life and briefly write about how this new command—loving as Jesus loved—specifically affects the way you're to love that person. Where does it push beyond what feels natural?

Turn back to 1 John 2:7-8. John explains that the commandment to love God and one another is something his readers had heard from the beginning. "The beginning" likely refers to the beginning of their Christian faith, from when they came into a saving relationship with Jesus. In effect John is saying that the command is old in that it's ancient in nature and his friends have known it for a while now, so he's not telling them anything new. On the other hand, the love command is new and he tells us why in verse 8: The darkness is fading and the real light is already shining. (This is one of those occasions where I don't feel smart enough for John—I'm back to trying to figure out how many hats people are wearing on the bus out of New York). Again, it will help to turn to John's Gospel for a better understanding.

Turn to John's Gospel and read 3:16-21. According to this passage, who is the Light that has come into the world?

Jesus

Reread 1 John 2:8 (margin). What is "realized" in both Jesus and us?

truth - True Light

Let's try to put this together. Now that Jesus has entered the world (Light into darkness) we can love our neighbors as ourselves more fully than we ever imagined! Why? Because the old commandment to love has now been revitalized and energized because of Christ (the new law). The new ability to love dwells in Him and also in us. The old command to love God and love others has now been pumped full of new life, which is being realized in Jesus and also in us (see v. 8).

PERSONAL TAKE: Summarizing this information from verse 8, explain why the old commandment is now new.

Light...

Now let's actually see how Jesus made an old command—love others as yourself—palpably new. Read John 13:1-5, 12-17. Keep in mind that John's feet were two of the ones Jesus washed.

In John 13:14-15, what did Jesus tell His disciples?

"do AS I do"

PERSONAL TAKE: Describe how Jesus made the old command to love one another new in this instance. There's no "right" answer, just your thoughts about how Jesus lived this command in a fresh way, and asks us to do the same.

An EXAMple was Set...

I read this passage while visiting a friend who was struggling with issues she'd dealt with for years. I find that patience is at a premium when encouraging people who battle the same things season after season. (Somehow I'm not nearly as bothered when I'm that person.) Anyhow, my inclination at the top of the week was to instruct, exhort, and lay out a plan of action. But the Lord spoke to me. "Just wash her feet. That's all I'm asking you to do." In this instance literal foot washing would have been totally lost on my friend and not at all what she needed (huge sigh of relief). Rather, the Lord was asking me to serve her, to lay down my agenda, to listen, to patiently tend to her. Over the course of that week the Lord enabled me to live the old command of loving my friend in a

"On the other hand, I am writing to you about a new law—and this is realized in him and also in you—because the darkness is fading, and the real light is already shining."[12]

The new command to love is loving like Jesus loved (1 John 2:7-8)

new way. Why was it new? Well, partly it was new because Christ's love was being realized in me in that present moment (see 1 John 2:8). Put in more technical terms: "The command to love is 'new' in its association with Jesus and also in its need to be constantly fulfilled in the experience of the Christian disciple."[13]

John has given us a piece of theology that is about to play an enormously practical role in our lives. He connects the Light of Christ in us to what he's about to say next.

Read 1 John 2:9-11. Do the activity in the margin.

John paints a strong picture for us here with vibrant imagery. In fact, his language is so strong that I don't want us to miss any conviction the Holy Spirit is bringing us. Hating a brother or sister in Christ can cause us to stumble around in the darkness. It blinds us in our ability to know where we're going in life, leaving us unable to hear clearly from the Lord.

When I think of the word *hate*, it's easy for me to let myself off the hook, thinking, *good thing I don't hate anyone*. But given the severity of John's charge, let's ask the Lord to show us any area where we may have hate in our hearts, or be on the road to hate. The road to hate can look like the enjoyment of gossip about someone you know, a thread of bitterness toward a family member, jealousy toward your coworker; it can even look like being sexually immoral with someone you claim to love.

> **PERSONAL REFLECTION:** Confess any areas the Lord shows you and write them below (always keeping in mind 1 John 1:9).

John is not only calling us to the absence of hate, but to a life overflowing with love for the people around us. As my pastor Jim likes to say, the Christian life is not only about the brake pedal, it's about the accelerator, too! Let's love today. Tangibly, practically, and in ways that push us to love like Jesus did. Let's allow the old command to be a new one because we're living it today. Reuben Welch, who wrote a book about community based on 1 John, says: "What I am sharing with you is both old and new. It is old in that it is the Word of the Bible and it has been true for a long time. It is new because the old truth has met me in the context of my personal journey and is changing my life."[14] Amen and Amen.

List all the benefits that accompany love and the snares that accompany hate under the corresponding heading

LOVE

Live in the Light
does not stumble

HATE

Walks in darkness
Does not Know where
he is going.
Blinded

DAY 4
I WRITE TO YOU

Someone said that comparison thinking leaves us feeling either smug or small—neither appealing results—and yet it comes to us so naturally. Even spiritually we compare ourselves, believing God only speaks to the people with seminary degrees or radical testimonies or big families or single missionaries. "I look at other people's relationship with God and wonder, *How can I have that relationship?*," a younger friend of mine asked me. "Sometimes you feel like you're never going to get there." We all feel this way at different times, which is why I love that John is about to single out varying stages of our faith journey, making sure he includes us all wherever we may be along the road. You're going to be so moved by his pastoral care, his zeal for each one of us to be included, his passion for not one of us to feel left out. He is renewing my love for the gospel all over again.

John R. Stott says, "John has abruptly concluded his exposition … He does not mean to give his readers the impression that he thinks they are in darkness or that he doubts the reality of their Christian faith … he digresses to tell them his view of their Christian standing. His purpose in writing is as much to confirm the right assurance of genuine Christians as to rob the counterfeit of their false assurance."[15]

Read 1 John 2:12-14.

In the table below list the reasons John is writing to each group:

Dear Children	Fathers	Young Men
Sins forgiven	Known him from beginning	over come the evil one
you have Known Father	Known him from beginning	Strong word of God lives in you
		overcome the evil one.

We don't know whether John is using these titles to refer to actual age or spiritual maturity. He may be using *children* to refer to all of his readers while then separating out the older in faith or age from the younger. Several interesting opinions exist, and I wish I could offer an absolute explanation. The good news is that the message is not lost despite the lack of clarity in this instance, and John's emphatic desire to encourage his readers in all stages of life and faith comes across clearly.

We can ultimately distill John's list down to three statements. Let's look at each one. He says he is writing because …

1. YOUR SINS HAVE BEEN FORGIVEN.

On what basis are our sins forgiven?

- ☐ our good deeds
- ☑ Jesus' name
- ☐ our religious sacrifices
- ☐ our innocence

I am still so prone to trying to earn forgiveness, thinking that if I work hard enough in a certain area to please God, He'll repay me by dismissing those other more troublesome areas. I love that John reminds us God's forgiveness doesn't rest on us. It rests fully on Jesus' name, which "represents both his person and saving work."[16] Psalm 51 clearly pictures how our cleansing is based on God's work, not ours.

Read Psalm 51:1-2,7-9,16-17 and list the visuals David uses to describe how God cleanses our hearts.

Unfailing Love   *Cleanse*   *Broken Spirit*
Great Compassion   *wash me*   *Broken & Contrite heart*
Blot out, wash away, cleanse   *Hide your face from my sin*

PERSONAL REFLECTION: In what ways do you try to earn God's forgiveness? How do 1 John 2:12 and Psalm 51 help you more fully rest in Jesus' saving work?

2. YOU HAVE KNOWN HIM FROM THE BEGINNING.

Turn to John's Gospel, verses 10:11-15. What does Jesus specifically intend for His "sheep" (children) in verse 14?

Know Him

Now turn to John 14:1-10. What question does Jesus ask Philip in verse 9?

Don't you Know me even After I have been around you for a long time

I love the raw texture of this passage, how human it is. After being with Jesus for "such a long time" Philip still doesn't fully know Him. I can hear the yearning in Jesus' voice, the compassion mingled with a possible hint of holy exasperation, longing for Philip to understand who He is.

This passage became clearer for me in the context of a relationship with an impoverished couple I'd befriended. We'd been working together for several months to get the necessary medical help for one of their children. After making great progress I was blindsided by a phone call from the mother who questioned my motives for helping. I was so taken off guard I could barely speak. After months of trying to get her child the help she needed, all I could say was, "Don't you know me by now?" Ultimately we were able to work it out, but as soon as I hung up the phone I knew the Lord had something deeper for me. He gently showed me how often I doubt or question His goodness after all He has been to me. I am certain there are times when the Lord is thinking, *Kelly, don't you know Me by now?*

> **PERSONAL TAKE:** How did Philip know Jesus yet not know Him, and how is this true of your own relationship with Christ?

3. YOU HAVE OVERCOME THE EVIL ONE.

> We'll look more fully at the theme of overcoming in the weeks ahead, but for now what two other descriptions does John give in the second half of 1 John 2:14 that seem connected to our ability to overcome the Evil One? "You are _Strong_____, and the _Word____ of God remains/lives in _you_."

We can think of God's Word as being His words, will, and way. Here we see that living by God's Word is inextricably connected to our strength to overcome. I meet so many people who are stuck in unrelenting misery, broken relationships, even tragic situations because they're committed to doing things their way instead of being led by the Word of God that abides in them. Simply put, living by God's Word is power over our Adversary.

Simply put, living by God's Word is power over our Adversary.

> We've already turned to Psalm 119 once this week and I want to go back there. I know you want to skip looking up all these verses, but push yourself. Beside each verse write how God's instructions are connected to overcoming:

> Psalm 119:11 *hid his word in our heart that I may Not Sin against him —*
>
> Psalm 119:24 *Your Statuates are my delight and counselors*

Psalm 119:25 *Preserve my life according to your word*

Psalm 119:28 *Strengthen me according to your Word*

Psalm 119:92 *The Law has been my delight - or I would have perished in my Affliction -*

Psalm 119:107 *Preserve my Life according to your word*

Psalm 119:153 *deliver me from my Suffering for I have not forgotten your word*

Psalm 119:165 *Great peace for those who Love your Law / Con't Stumble*

Psalm 119:173 *may your hand help me for I have chosen your precepts -*

Quickly flip to John's Gospel, 8:37. In this instance, how were the Jews to whom Jesus was speaking treating His Word?

You have no room for my word

PERSONAL RESPONSE: Is there any area where you have not made room for the will and way of God that may be keeping you from overcoming? Take time to consider and respond.

I've been waiting all day to get to this next part: 1 John 2:12-14 are written in the—wait for it—perfect indicative! I know. You never thought Bible study could be so fun. Seriously, you're going to love these two words when we're done with them. The *perfect indicative* means *an action that's already completed,* as well as *an objective fact or reality.*

So when John writes that our sins have been forgiven, that we've known God and that we've overcome the Evil One, he's saying that these are factual realities that have already been accomplished! As many have said, the perfect indicative gives "the mood of certainty." How assuring for the ancient words of John to greet us with more certainty than the rising sun. Because of Jesus we have been forgiven (perfect tense), we have come to know God (perfect tense), we have overcome (perfect tense).

I don't know what kind of family you grew up in, if you had encouraging parents or belittling ones, if your home was whole or broken. I don't know what words were spoken over you, words of empowerment or degradation. What I do know is that most of us at some point feel weak and powerless, caught in a cycle of habitual struggles we don't foresee ever rising above. To you, I reiterate John's words "you are strong." You're way stronger than you think. You're strong to overcome because you have the Word of God. Don't believe the lie that you're weak. You're not.

If you're a believer in Christ, write the words "I am strong" with confidence in the space below. If you feel a little ridiculous doing so, all the more reason to write it.

DAY 5

LIVING FOR WHAT LASTS

I'm a homeowner of a 1930s cottage and the home's age has required all manner of plumbers, chimney sweepers, roofers, structural engineers, glaziers for the old glass in my windows, to tromp through my house. Despite the need for upkeep, the one phrase I repeatedly hear is, "Ma'am, this house is solid as a rock." Followed up with, "They sure don't make 'em like they used to." And they're right about that. Cedar logs nearly a century old are holding my house upright. The blown glass windowpanes are all original and so is the cedar shake that has somehow outlasted the aluminum siding on the street. I don't even understand it. I just know that quality and endurance are characteristics we seem a little thin on these days—a sentence that alarmingly just rolled off my fingertips like I'm 82. As we look at the next few verses, be thinking about how the prize of longevity plays into John's exhortations.

Read 1 John 2:15-17.

In verses 15-17, John moves from the perfect indicative (verses 12-15) to the present imperative—I knew you would want to know this.

From memory, what is the perfect indicative? (Look back at yesterday's lesson if you need to.)

An action already Completed

The present imperative, on the other hand, is a call to action either negative or positive (stop doing this/start doing that). We tend to bow up at imperatives, especially in our modern age, mostly because we don't want to be told what to do or not do. In some ways we seem more comfortable when life is vague and blurry and gray, mostly so we can choose for ourselves. The question is, at what cost?

Before really digging into John's imperatives, I first want to make the connection between yesterday's verses and today's. John is giving us today's imperatives because of yesterday's indicatives. More simply put, because of God's perfect, complete work (vv. 12-14), we now have a responsibility (v. 15-17). It's like this: Perfect Indicative—The apple pie just came out of the oven (completed action); Present Imperative—Sit down and eat a piece (your call to action).

> Because of God's perfect, complete work (vv. 12-14), we now have a responsibility (vv. 15-17).

What two things does John tell us not to love in verse 15? (I've filled in the first one for you).

1. The world

2. ___*Anything*___ ___*in*___ the world

A definition of the word *world* is important here because of how many different meanings the word can have. After researching several definitions and descriptions, I really like scholar Stephen Smalley's take: John is saying don't love "human society, temporarily controlled by the power of evil, organized in opposition to God."[17] John doesn't mean don't love the earth itself or its people: "There is no suggestion that the Christian is to hate the material world or its inhabitants."[18] The very fact that Jesus took on flesh and came to earth to redeem us demonstrates His love for the material world.

PERSONAL TAKE: How do verses 16-17 help interpret verse 15? In other words, how do the things that belong to the world and their qualities (vv. 16-17) fuel John's command for us not to love the world in verse 15? Take some time with this.

Cravings of sinful man
Lust of his eyes
boasting of what he has & does

I used to get these verses all confused because I would take verse 15 as separate from verses 16 and 17. I would wrongly assume that I had to stop loving the beach, ice cream, music, reading, the desire for intimacy, even some people. I couldn't for the life of me understand why God would put us in the world and then tell us not to love it or anything in it. I'd even heard strict and joyless teachers try to persuade me that pleasure or enjoyment of most any kind were ungodly. This is where verses 16 and 17 come in, among others. For ease we're going to refer to the HCSB translation, but feel free to read your own as well.

"For everything that belongs to the world—the lust of the flesh, the lust of the eyes, and the pride in one's lifestyle—is not from the Father, but is from the world. And the world with its lust is passing away, but the one who does God's will remains forever." (1 John 2:16-17)

John uses three descriptions to define what belongs to the world (what he doesn't want us to love). List them below:

1. Cravings of sinful man
2. Lust of his eyes
3. boasting of what he has + does

Let's look at each of the three entities separately. We'll do our best not to get lost in splitting hairs between meanings, instead letting the broad truths speak to our hearts.

1. LUST OF THE FLESH

Some of your translations may render the first phrase "lust of the flesh" or "cravings of sinful man." I think what's key here is to see that John is not speaking of redeemed passions and desires, but the ones that originate apart from Christ.

A friend of mine recently went to see a famous performer who's a household name in concert. When the lights came up on the stage of the stadium the performer was on a two-story throne. She then proceeded to fly over the audience from a harness while thousands screamed her name, reaching their hands toward her body. The best part is that this performer began her stunt by saying, "I do this for you." My friend was thinking, *and maybe the tiniest bit for herself.* This could probably fall under the lust of the flesh. Our desire to be exalted, or even worshiped.

The lust of the flesh can also refer to our craving revenge, desiring to be right more than valuing another person. It can mean hungering for morsels of gossip, fame at the expense of others, money and possessions no matter the cost of time away from family, friends, or people who need us. Our flesh can lust after over-eating, over-spending, excessive entertainment, and, yes, for sexual things like pornography, sex outside of marriage, an affair, etc. Activities we know do harm to ourselves, others, and our fellowship with God.

> **PERSONAL REFLECTION:** In your own words, describe an everyday example of the lust of the flesh that you personally encounter. What does a continual attempt to fill your lusts result in?

2. LUST OF THE EYES

We could point to several examples in Scripture of the lust of our eyes leading us down painful paths, but I chose one for us to consider.

> Read 2 Samuel 11:2-17. List the progressive steps of David's sin from the moment he saw Bathsheba from his rooftop (I filled in some for you).
>
> saw her ⟶ lusted after her ⟶ _____
>
> _____ ⟶ _____

I chose this example because this costly and complicated act of adultery began with a glance. I remember a pastor whom I love and respect tell me how exceedingly careful he is about what he allows himself to watch because "our eyesight is fragile." How true a statement this is. How often our eyesight will deceive us because "It will include 'the love of beauty,' " but will be " 'divorced from the law of goodness.' "[19]

Like Adam and Eve in the garden, there is immeasurable beauty and goodness to set our eyes upon. We don't have to degrade the gift of sight by pouring over what is cheap, depressing, sensual, or deceitful.

PERSONAL RESPONSE: What do you need to stop watching or reading? What wonderful things could you dwell on in its place?

3. PRIDE IN ONE'S LIFESTYLE

This one involves boasting of what we have and do. I'm trying to imagine how John would have treated this one in our day of posting, Tweeting, Instagramming, blogging, documenting, and uploading just about everything we own and everything we do. Social media can be a wonderful tool, but if our pride is like fire, social media is the wood that fuels it. And this includes all those posts that appear humble when really all we're doing is not being humble at all! Anyone?

PERSONAL REFLECTION: How would your social media presence change—be specific—if what you posted was meant to love others versus promoting your pride, position, accomplishments? (Don't get legalistic and don't judge others' motives. And if you're not a part of social media, simply pull the question into another area of your life.)

I'm glad John doesn't leave us with this list apart from further explanation. He gives specific reasons for why he warns against a fallen love of the world (as defined above) and the lusts that belong to the world.

First, from where do these three things originate? (v. 16)
in the World

What eventually happens to these desires? (v. 17)
Pass away –

Not only do these desires originate from a system that is not from God, but also one that is passing away. So, among other problems, the lust of the flesh, lust of the eyes, and the pride of life are simply really bad investments in the long-term. But, John says at the end of verse 17:

The one who does God's will ____*Lives*____ forever.

Speaking of the eternal, I can't help but have you briefly turn to Luke 10:38-42. According to verse 42 what did Jesus say about what Mary had chosen?

Mary has chosen what is better – + will Not be taken away from her.

We put way too much hope in this world, in this temporal, passing reality. Whereas the time we spend abiding in Jesus will never be taken from us. In the three verses we studied today John pleads with us not to spend our affections on what is evil and fleeting. Instead, the person who does His will, lives/remains/abides forever (depending on your translation). We'll talk much more about John's love for the word *remain* in coming days and in session 5. I'm excited to study this more closely, because I have always longed for a place of constancy. Jesus makes this possible.

PERSONAL RESPONSE: As we close Week 2, write down the most prominent truth or revelation you've encountered this week.

You've accomplished a lot this week. I commend you. 1 John is not the easiest book to understand and some of the concepts are deeply personal, sometimes uncomfortable.

You may be feeling genuine conviction because you know you're not walking in the ways God has directed. With passion, hope, and grace, my prayer is that you will walk in a way that is congruent with your love for Jesus. And for those who are continually plagued with guilt and condemnation, I want to leave you with a story.

While in the Amazon I heard a Brazilian pastor give three of the most refreshing and revelatory messages I've heard in a long time. After he spoke he personally shared about going through a devastating divorce where he lost his church in the process. Even after a few years of "Jesus treating him," as he put it, he confessed that when he stands up to teach he often has feelings of shame and condemnation over the fact that he's divorced. After he shared this with us a dear pastor friend of mine walked up to my new Brazilian friend, placed both hands on his shoulders, drew his face within an inch of his nose and with tears in his eyes said, "Brother, don't you ever let the Enemy rob you of your calling. You're a godly man and your past does not define you."

I wish I could place my hands on your shoulders and you could place your hands on mine and we could speak these words to one another. We won't do this life perfectly, and that's why we have an Advocate. At the same time, if we know Him, our lives will reflect who Jesus is and what He's about. May the Savior help you know that you know.

BLACK BEAN AND CHICKEN CHILI

FROM THE KITCHEN OF BETHANY B.

I love a good chili, especially one that doesn't sacrifice taste for health. Full of flavor and spices, and easy to throw together, this is a quick and healthy way to enjoy the classic comforts of chili. Add a dollop of sour cream along with chips and salsa as a side, and you've got Fall in a bowl.

INGREDIENTS:

- 2 large skinless, boneless chicken breasts cut into 1 inch cubes
- 3 & 1/3 cups water
- 1/2 can tomato paste *(6 oz)*
- 1 & 1/2 tablespoons cooking oil

SEASONING:

- ground sea salt *(to taste)*
- 1 tablespoon chili powder *(less or more to taste)*
- 1 teaspoon cumin
- ground black pepper *(to taste)*
- 1/4 teaspoon ground cayenne pepper

VEGETABLES:

- 1/2 yellow onion *(diced)*
- 1 medium green bell pepper *(diced) (OR use two small bell peppers)*
- 1 medium red bell pepper *(diced) (OR use two small bell peppers)*
- 1/2 jalapeno pepper, seeded and diced *(OR use 1/2 of one 4 oz can of diced jalapenos or diced green chili peppers)*
- 3 roma tomatoes *(diced) (OR use 1 can of diced tomatoes with or w/o green chili peppers mixed in.)*
- 1 can whole kernel corn *(drained) (approximately 15 oz)*
- 2 cans of black beans
- 2/3 bunch fresh cilantro, chopped

DIRECTIONS:

1. Heat oil in a large pot over medium heat.
2. Place chicken in pot until chicken is brown on all sides.
3. Mix all spices (salt, pepper, cumin, etc.) together and then add to the pot with chicken.
4. Mix in FRESH veggies (not canned) (bell peppers, etc.)
5. Pour in 1/2 of the water.
6. Cook for 10 minutes or until about 1/2 the water has evaporated.
7. Mix in CANNED veggies (black beans, corn, etc.)
8. Reduce to low heat and mix in remaining water.
9. Mix in tomato paste.
10. Simmer for 30 minutes or until thickened. stir occasionally.
11. To serve, top with chopped cilantro! Other topping options are shredded cheddar jack cheese and/ or sour cream. Eat with a spoon, or use blue corn tortilla chips to scoop up the chili instead of a spoon! Makes approximately 4-6 servings. Tastes great re-heated and can even be frozen.

CLASSIC CHOCOLATE CHIP COOKIES
FROM THE KITCHEN OF JAZZMINE W.

INGREDIENT LIST

- 3 cups all purpose flour
- 1 tsp baking soda
- 1 tsp salt
- 2 sticks butter, softened
- 3/4 cup granulated sugar
- 3/4 cup brown sugar
- 1 1/2 tsp vanilla
- 2 large eggs
- 2 cups of chocolate chips
- 1 cup chopped pecans

SECRET INGREDIENT:

- One dash cinnamon

RECIPE INSTRUCTIONS

1. Mix dry ingredients in a bowl and set aside.
2. Mix butter and sugar in a separate bowl.
3. Add eggs and vanilla.
4. Add dry ingredients.
5. Stir in chocolate chips and pecans.
6. Bake @350 for 15-18 minutes.

TO REMAIN

We talk about the courage needed to leave a place, the strength to move out into uncharted territories. We admire those who take to change like a boat to water, dipping their oar in for the next new adventure. This is the stuff of revolutions and gold rushes. But sometimes it takes just as much strength to stay put as it does to go. It's not easy facing the same dishes piled up in the same sink, the routine work week, the interminable annoying habits that of course you don't have but that the people around you use continually to sharpen your character.

Remaining takes commitment. It puts up with the mundane. It chooses to love even when the glow of newness has faded. Remaining knows the value of longevity, loyalty, and hard work that eventually pays off. To remain is to know your labor is not in vain. It's to live with hope.

If we were to wake up in John's era we would witness an upheaval from within the church, new and vogue ideas about Jesus were circulating—ideas contrary to what had been taught from the beginning. We'd see people leaving the church for "higher" enlightenment, attempting to pull others with them.

In response to all the tumult, John's plea was simple: Remain. Dwell. Abide. Don't leave the steadying truth that you know for the sparkle of nouveau philosophies or the swell of cultural tides. Remain within Jesus and the fellowship of His Bride.

The practice of abiding is never more difficult than when we're surrounded by a host of other vines from which a lot of bubbly people are hanging—all happy in their flesh and darkness. You know, when everyone else's vine appears more thrilling than the one you're attached to. You look around and begin to believe the lies of the Enemy—that the way of Jesus is limiting and that His followers are outdated.

Suddenly you have this overwhelming pull to tie your branch up to that new belief system, the married man who's showing you attention, the higher-paying job that'll take you away from your children, the extra drink, the glance at pornography. We deceive ourselves into thinking new, interesting branches will offer more nourishment, so we spend our time hopping from vine to vine, looking for another place to dwell.

At certain points in my life the idea of remaining in Jesus felt like death. And, I suppose it was death—death to self, which is the good kind. Higher learning was calling, the air was redolent with the pride of life, intoxicating personalities laden with charisma and allure were calling my name—and they liked me. But none of this "newness" was about the stuff I'd known from the beginning. The people I was drawn to weren't abiding in the Vine, rather they had made up their own rules and were enjoying living by them.

For a season I toyed with what it might look like to try to play in both places; a toe in the church and my heart in the world, but this is not what abiding means. Rather, such a lifestyle means a crack down the center of your being. Ultimately I couldn't live torn like that for reasons that have a whole lot to do with the passages and doctrines we're going to study this week about the mystery of abiding in Christ and Christ abiding in us. Because of this truth the Lord never let me break away, and I'm forever indebted to Him. Praise God for us in Him, and He in us, the latter being the more powerful of the two.

Perhaps you are in a similar position. You're wondering if that which was from the beginning, this message of the gospel, is really all it promises to be. The Christian fundamentals you've known seem tired while the lust of the flesh appears to gallop across open fields with vigor and excitement.

But as we'll see this week, the anointing that the world boasts of is counterfeit, and it's fleeting. It is not the real thing, which is why we'll hear John communicate with passion, "Do not let anyone deceive you." Because there are deceivers out there and people get deceived. And one of John's greatest passions was to keep the fellowship of the community intact, reminding his church that constancy in Christ far outweighs the temporal electricity of those who'd moved on for more "enlightening" ideas.

As I grow older, the more my heart yearns for stability. Not stagnancy, mind you— rather, immutability. I long for what will never change, all that's constant in Jesus, promises that never fail, fellowship that will carry on for as long as forever. In a world of ceaseless change and dissenting opinions, how grounding it is to know that we can know. Especially when social spheres, media, and culture tirelessly seek to persuade us to question our faith, to doubt God's truth, to adhere to His Word selectively.

I can nearly hear John calling out to his readers, "Dear little children, don't let the deceiving voices make you doubt what you know! You know His truth. You've confessed the Son and so you have the Father as well. Remain right where you are. This is your home. I know the voices are familiar, people who were once close to you. But don't forsake what you've heard from the beginning—the gospel that rung so true the moment you heard it, the moment it changed you."

VIEWER GUIDE

WALKING IN THE LIGHT

GROUP DISCUSSION QUESTIONS:

What was the most impacting moment for you this week (in video or print study)?

Turn to Isaiah 5:20 and discuss specific examples in your daily environment of light being cast as darkness and darkness being cast as light. How do you discern what is true darkness and true light?

Kelly spoke about the interesting reality that fellowship with one another is a direct result of walking in God's light (1 John 1:7). How have you seen this play out in your own life where walking in the light of obedience opened up deeper fellowship with others?

How has seeing Christ as your Advocate and the propitiation for your sins taken your love and appreciation for Him to a deeper place? (p. 43)

John writes about our sins being forgiven as an action that's already been completed through Christ (perfect indicative). At what points in your life do you struggle to believe you really have been forgiven? (p. 57)

WHEN THINGS CHANGE

I've been gardening for the past few years, each spring yielding another reason for another horticultural project. My inner farmer officially reached new heights this year with my latest addition—my friend Daniel built me two 4-by-4 cedar compost bins built for excess kitchen scraps, grass clippings, fall leaves, last year's okra vines. I've been reading up on the carbon/nitrogen balance of composting and the fastest way for say, an egg shell or an eggplant or the day's coffee grounds to turn into this magical fairy dust that makes everything in your garden come bounding out of the earth with glee. Scientists prefer to call this wonder dust *humus*.

While reading up on composting, I started to get lost in the math and science of it all, when what I really wanted from my compost pile was better dirt to make a better cucumber. I wanted food, not a science lesson—practical, not technical. But the reality is that I need both. If I'm going to compost correctly for a good harvest—and I will figure this out—understanding a little something of the scientific elements of heat, airflow, microbes, and compounds will help me obtain the soil I'm looking for. Which will help me with the better tomato. I know … this is the saddest intro to a Bible study week you've ever read, but humor me.

First, Second, and Third John are heavy theologically, and at times a bit technical. I'll keep reminding you, as I remind myself, that John's passion for his readers is intensely personal and ultimately practical. But sometimes it takes us breaking down words, digging into definitions, and pulling apart weighty doctrinal truths to get to what we can apply to our difficult marriage, our lonely singleness, or our painful time of waiting. Some of what we learn may not be readily applied to our current situations directly, but we'll understand something significant about our great God and the way He's saved us and how He loves us. We'll find how good it is for us to take our eyes off our pressing pains and lose ourselves in the vastness and wonder of God and the Christian faith. Not everything is about our immediate needs or circumstances or zucchini. So, with that … welcome to week 3.

As we open a new set of verses, a little background is important. You'll notice John uses the term *Antichrist* as well as *antichrists*. I can tell you're excited. The former refers to a specific individual who will appear during the very last days and feign to be the Messiah. The latter refers to several antichrists who have already come. These antichrists weren't claiming to be Jesus, but in the spirit of the Antichrist, they were propagating false ideas about Jesus and threatened to deceive members of the church. John is the only one who uses the term *antichrist,* though the concept is found elsewhere in Scripture. (See 2 Thess. 2:1-12.) Okay, I've already over-written, so now it's your turn to read and ponder.

Read 1 John 2:18-22. According to verse 22 a chief truth of Jesus' divinity was in question: The antichrists denied that He was …

- ❏ the Prince of Peace
- ❏ the King of the Jews
- ☑ the Christ/Messiah
- ❏ Melchizedek

What else did these deceivers deny about Jesus (see 2 John 7)?

TRUE/FALSE. John and his community departed from the false teachers (v. 19).

denies the father & the Son —

The title *Christ* or *Messiah* means *Anointed One.* It is a term virtually equivalent to saying *the very Son of God.* While some rejected His divinity, others denied He had come in the flesh (the incarnation). There may have been other forms of denial, but the significant point for us to consider is that the division centered on the person of Jesus and who He claimed to be. We will end Week 5 with more on the humanity and divinity of Christ. For now, simply remember that Jesus being both fully human and fully God is essential to the Christian faith, and a truth for which John contended.

Read the Gospel of John 7:37-43. What one word in verse 43 describes the effect of the differing beliefs people had about Jesus?

divided

How is Jesus related to God the Father (see John 12:44-45)?

Believe in Jesus - Believe in the father

When I read terms like *deceivers, false prophets,* and *antichrists,* I tend to picture a bunch of hooligans running around in black masks and capes. But that would be entirely too obvious to identify and not at all what John is describing here.

According to 1 John 2:19, how closely related to John's readers can you infer this community was at one time?

went out from us … did not really belong to us.

PERSONAL TAKE: Glance at 1 John 2:26, 1 John 4:1, and 2 John 7, and notice the danger these individuals posed. Now really consider this: How might the fact that these antichrists were at one time a part of John's community make the division and false claims all the more difficult to handle?

Those trying to lead you astray – do not believe every Spirit
Those that do not acknowledge Jesus Christ as coming in the flesh is a deceiver

John uses a distinct phrase at the top of verse 19, "they went out from us." While there may be times when God calls us to break relationship with someone or a group of people, these particular dissenters had "gone out" from the community. They were the ones who had left. The news is sad because many of us have known people over the years—people dear to us—who no longer claim Jesus. Or, perhaps they still claim Him but are not living in the light or walking according to His Word. Some of these people may have been dear friends, perhaps even spouses or children who have left the community of faith.

Though John is clear that this group of secessionists never really belonged to the community in the first place—otherwise they would have remained—at one point these people surely felt to the church community like they belonged. This picture hits much closer to home and is more painful than the idea of watching out for really obvious dissenters from the outside. The perplexing loss of people we were once close to is much more heartbreaking. While John doesn't mention his sadness here, I can attest to my own. I can't think of anything in my life that has caused me more grief than the loss of relationship over friends turning away from God's will and way.

> **PERSONAL REFLECTION:** Without leaving anything potentially harmful on the page, has your belief in Jesus and your commitment to Him ever been the cause of a friendship that eventually drifted apart? If you can pinpoint it, what about Jesus or your faith caused the separation? Respond in the margin.

One of the main reasons John wrote was to protect the true members of the church from being led astray (v. 26). His concerns are no less valid today, perhaps even more so as the temptation to latch onto the latest trend or persuasive argument still exists—even if these are ancient deceptions dressed in modern clothing.

Because these voices have at times gotten to me, and because the Lord has used severe mercy in my life to pull me from deceptive people and ways of thinking, I hope you will feel my passion for you coursing through the last part of today's study.

Read 2 Timothy 3:1-7. Verse 7 describes a curious combination.
The people were always __Learning__
But they never acknowledged the __truth__

Read 2 Timothy 4:3. For what two reasons does Paul suggest people will turn away from the truth?
Suit their own Desires
gather around Them a great Number of teachers to say what their

What were the Athenians spending their time doing in Acts 17:21? *Itching ears want to hear.*

Spent their time doing nothing / talking + Listening
To the Latest ideas.
What current ideas or cultural tides have caused you to question any part of (1) the gospel message, (2) Jesus' teaching, (3) the soundness of God's Word? Be honest in your answers since the Lord already knows your thoughts. Respond in the margin.

Sometimes our faith wanes because we've been blindsided by a tragedy. Other times it's because we can't reconcile a particular truth of God's Word—or what we mistakenly think God's Word says about a subject—with a certain circumstance or reality. But most of the time if we're honest our doubts and questions flow out of our wayward passions and lusts. In other words, we want what we want and we'll find whatever "truth" will back us up—I certainly have experienced this. So here's what I want you to consider:

PERSONAL REFLECTION: If you're doubting your faith or struggling with obedience to God's Word, consider the verses you read as expressed in the descriptions below. Honestly ask yourself if any of these reflect your current state and write your thoughts beside the description that best describes you.

• I have an obsession with learning but I don't really want the truth—I don't really want to "get well." (See 2 Tim. 3:1-7.)

• I want to follow my personal desires and passions even though they're contrary to a road of obedience. (See 2 Tim. 4:3.)

• I find myself listening to and searching after "teachers" I want to hear versus what Scripture reveals. (See Acts 17:2; 2 Tim. 4:3.)

As noted earlier, the gnostics or pre-gnostics of John's day claimed that enlightenment and freedom came through a special knowledge of God rather than obedience to Jesus. Today we have similarly deceptive messages like "follow your heart," "do what feels good to you," "live and let live," "the Bible is a nice book but flawed." These all are enormously attractive ideas in the moment because they give the illusion that we're free to do and believe what we want. But life, joy, peace, prosperity come through the unbending, unshakable truth of Christ and God's Word.

Freedom lives in the blessed confines of obedience. Dear reader, don't be deceived by the rampant voices—even the smart and thoughtful and sympathetic ones—if they don't fall against the plumb line of God's truth revealed in Scripture. Don't offer up what you know to be true at the altar of your fleeting lusts and fickle desires. He is so much more. In the words of John, "I do not write to you because you do not know the truth, but because you do know it" (1 John 2:21). Resolve to live like what you know.

DAY 2
WHAT STAYS THE SAME

I hear more voices, opinions, discoveries, and studies than ever, and I can't keep up. Oatmeal used to be a super food, now it's a dastardly grain. Butter was awesome, then it was the worst thing ever—like pouring sludge straight in your veins—so we all jumped on the margarine bandwagon until we hit the pothole of hydrogenated oil and realized it's even worse than the sludge, so we're back to butter and it's amazing fat properties, of all things. Do you nurse or use formula, get the epidural, or go for all-natural excruciation? Should you public school, private school, or homeschool the kids? With mommy blogs, online sermons, DIY shows, medical help sites, and breaking discoveries, the information is inexhaustible. Even if you narrow it down to "Christian" resources, you still have an ocean of material, much of it conflicting.

So what do you do besides throw your hands up in total exasperation, deciding that somewhere someone has deemed pizza, french fries, and a milkshake to be a shockingly nutritious meal—this just in—and drown yourself in calories amidst the thought that you can never truly know anything? I think this is why I'm so ready for John's words today. You really can know a few things, some truths don't change.

Read 1 John 2:18-29, repeating part of yesterday's reading.

Yesterday we focused on the secessionists who had left the community and the warnings about deceivers. Today we'll concentrate on the wealth of assurance John brings to those who have faithfully remained. Notice how John's letter dramatically turns in verse 20 from warning to affirmation: Almost every translation begins with "But you." (Except the King James is "but ye," of which I'm particularly fond.) John is saying, Dear child, things are different for you.

> Briefly note what two positive realities are true about the believers he's writing to, as opposed to the antichrists.
> 1. You have an __anointing__ from the Holy One (v. 20)
> 2. You know the __truth__ (v. 21)

We'll talk about the amazing implications of anointing tomorrow, for now recognize that no matter the shame of your past, the questions of your present or the worries of your future, if you are in Christ, John is affirming you: You have a special anointing, because you know the truth!

PERSONAL REFLECTION: How does this encourage you?

> A key word appears in verses 19, 24, 27 and 28. Because of differing translations, you may see slightly different words used. Fill in whatever word(s) your Bible uses. I've made the phrases generic enough so you can determine the proper word.
>
> v. 19: If the people who left had belonged to us, they would have __Remained__ with us.
>
> v. 24: What you've heard from the beginning must __remains__ in you. If it does __remain__ in you, you will __remain__ in the Son and in the Father.
>
> v. 27: The anointing you've received from Him __remain__ in you … Just as He has taught you, __remain__ in Him.
>
> v. 28: Little children, __Continue__ in Him.

Every believer in Christ has an anointing from the Holy One (1 John 2:20,27)

Though different English words are used at different times depending on your translation, they all derive from the same Greek word *meno,* which can mean: "not to depart; to continue, to be present; to be held, kept, continually; to continue to be, not to perish, to last, endure."[1] Or from Strong's concordance: "to stay (in a given place, state, relation or expectancy)."[2] Read those definitions again slowly.

And then once more even slower.

> **PERSONAL REFLECTION:** In a world where so much is changing and in constant flux, what part of the definition of *meno* means the most to you and why? (Also, consider the context in which John is using the word.)

We really can't do justice to today's passage in 1 John without turning to John's Gospel where Jesus further describes this idea of what it means to *meno* in Him. To help us understand He points to an example in nature that every reader would have been well acquainted with at the time: He takes us to the grapevine.

> Turn to John's Gospel and read verses 15:1-8. Take in every usage of the word *remain/abide/dwell*. According to verses 4 and 5, who is to remain in whom? (Note: this a two-part answer.)
>
> *Remain in me and I will remain in you*
>
> **PERSONAL TAKE:** From a strictly natural point of view, why can the branch do nothing apart from the vine? Think high school earth science.

One of the first lessons I learned when gardening is how dependent the branches (or in my case, stems) are to the vine. My first true gardening heartache came one morning when I jerked the water hose toward me accidentally decapitating one of my prize heirloom pepper plants. My gardening friend Mark was the only person in my community willing to mourn a bell pepper with me. Bless him. Within a few hours the fruit on the lopped off part of the plant had shriveled and the once green healthy stem was limp and lifeless. This is such an obvious spiritual lesson we tend to overlook: We can have no life apart from the life of Jesus. To truly live and bear fruit we have to *meno* in Him.

PERSONAL REFLECTION: Is there anything you are trying to accomplish right now as a lone branch apart from the true vine of Jesus? If so, explain.

PERSONAL RESPONSE: Keeping this exact situation in mind, what would choosing to abide in Him mean or require?

Now turn back to 1 John 2:24. What interesting thing does John tell us to make sure *menos* in us?

Remain in the Son & the father.

What they heard from the beginning is widely accepted as the preaching of the Christian Gospel.[3] In light of those who had walked away from the truth of Jesus, John was encouraging his people to let the transforming message of salvation in Christ remain *(meno)* in them. Frankly, this can be confusing because John later mentions that the anointing already remains in the believer, but here he is encouraging us to make sure the message of the gospel remains in us. We also read in John 15 how Jesus says He abides in us but how we're also to abide in Him.

I would like to relieve you—and myself—of all tension here, offering you something along the lines of: Jesus abides in us, we don't have to do another thing, end of story. But both Jesus and John seem to offer something that is more mutual in nature. Acording to 1 John, we truly do have a responsibility to abide in Christ, and to make sure the purity of Christ's message remains in us.

I don't believe John is saying that salvation comes by how hard we cling to this message. Remember that the message they'd heard from the beginning is the good news that God clings to us by sending Jesus in the flesh to save us apart from any of our good works. When this message dwells in you, you also dwell in the Son and Father and have the promise of eternal life. So don't read earning your salvation into this. Period.

At the same time, allow the tension to pull at you wherever it's pulling: We have a responsibility to allow the good news of Jesus, rooted in Scripture, to abide in us richly and in a way that will literally affect the way we live our lives. We need to actively foster this message of hope and truth in our hearts.*

> **PERSONAL RESPONSE:** We can take many practical steps to ensure that the truth of the gospel remains in us: fellowship, prayer, studying God's Word, learning under a pastor, just to name a few. Since you most likely know these, let me come at this from a different angle: What are some of the activities, social circles, entertainment, habits that hinder the gospel message from abiding deeply in you?
>
> In verse 26, what reason does John give for encouraging the message of truth to remain in his readers?
> ☑ Deceivers were trying to lead the believers astray.
> ❏ He wanted to bring the believers closer to God.
> ❏ So the believers could pass a theological test.

The scene John described in this chapter may be just the one you're living today. The message of the revealed truth of Christ might have dimmed to but a flicker in your heart while the flame of new ideas, higher-thinking, and all-encompassing acceptance is the most attractive. John says foster the message that's from the beginning. The message of Jesus. Go back to His Word. His teachings. The truth you know.

The beauty of the good news of the gospel is that "it had not changed and would not change" and will not change.[4] No New York Times Best Seller or persuasive personality can argue it away. You never have to worry about it being suddenly upended by a shocking new discovery, a learned professor, or a scientific breakthrough.

The message that Jesus preached about Himself cannot, by its very nature, be mingled, mixed, or swirled with other religious leaders or movements, because salvation rests solely on Jesus' coming to earth in human flesh (the incarnation), His death, and resurrection that we might be reconciled to God. Some things still remain.

*In showing that this verse is not a condition for our salvation but a reality of it, when John restates in verse 24 that "if the message does remain in you…", Smalley writes, "the restatement is in the form of a condition and anticipates a situation in which the challenge of v. 24a has been met. If the believer appropriates the Christian message, a relationship with God in Christ is the result (v24c)."[5]

DAY 3

THE CHRISMA

Growing up in the church I was blessed to know many men and women in whom the light of Jesus beamed, even in the most trying circumstances. I grew up hearing from missionaries who'd left comfortable lives for difficult parts of the world. I watched dear friends of our family lose their twelve year-old son to Leukemia. They suffered beyond words but they suffered with faith and hope and, even at times, joy. I knew women who were betrayed by their husbands yet who demonstrated amazing forgiveness, regardless of whether or not their marriages survived.

These kinds of stories don't tend to show up when scrutinizing the facts of Christianity. But some of the greatest apologetics of the Christian faith are the things that don't make it into the textbooks—it's the intangible of ordinary people walking through life in extraordinary, Christlike measures. I couldn't be any more excited about today's study because John gives us a glimpse as to what this intangible is, and how every believer in Jesus has been touched by it.

Read 1 John 2:20-29. In verse 20 what does John say we have?

Anointing —

According to verse 27, does John describe this as something a person earns or is given?

Anointing

Let's look at the definition of *chrisma*, the Greek word for *anointing*: "anything smeared on, unguent, ointment, usually prepared by the Hebrews from oil and aromatic herbs. Anointing was the inaugural ceremony for priests."[6] John is the only one who uses this exact Greek word, and since his usage is unique, I want to look at some Old Testament examples of anointing. This will help us better understand how John is using the term in 1 John 2:20 and 27.

In the margin briefly detail what made up the anointing substance according to Exodus 30:22-33. Who was the anointing exclusively for? (v. 30)

Priests

1 Samuel 16:1-13: For what office was David anointed?

King

chrisma, the Greek word for *anointing:* "anything smeared on, unguent, ointment, usually prepared by the Hebrews from oil and aromatic herbs. Anointing was the inaugural ceremony for priests."[6]

Isaiah 61:1-3. Who anointed Jesus and for what purpose?

We learn from these passages that persons in the Old Testament were anointed to set them apart for sacred use. Priests were anointed for the duty of the priesthood. The shepherd boy, David, was anointed for kingship. Even Jesus was anointed, by the Lord, for His earthly ministry. In these instances the anointing was similar to an initiation or consecration that involved a defining moment, a setting apart for a sacred purpose.

Now turn back 1 John 2:20: From whom does our anointing come?

Holy One —

The unique element of the anointing John speaks of is that this *chrisma* isn't oil from a place or a bottle, but an anointing from Jesus Himself. The moment we come into saving relationship with Jesus, He literally anoints or consecrates us. John "seems to be describing an initial moment of conversion or commitment to Christ."[7]

PERSONAL REFLECTION: After reading a bit about the process, have you ever considered your anointing? What does this mean to you that Jesus, the Holy One, has set you apart with His *chrisma*?

I want to explore more about this amazing word *chrisma* with you. See the verses below, two of which you've already read. In each reference, what member of the Trinity is associated with the anointing?

ISAIAH 61:1 *"The Spirit of the Sovereign LORD is on me because the LORD has anointed me..."*

1 SAMUEL 16:13 *"So Samuel took the horn of oil and anointed him ... the Spirit of the LORD came powerfully upon David."*

ACTS 10:38 *"God anointed Jesus of Nazareth with the Holy Spirit"*

2 CORINTHIANS 1:21-22 *"He anointed us, set his seal of ownership on us, and put his Spirit in our hearts as a deposit, guaranteeing what is to come."*

Many scholars believe that the anointing is the reception of the Holy Spirit. Others believe the anointing includes both the Holy Spirit and God's Word (see Eph. 1:13-14 compared with 1 John 2:27).

The secessionists were claiming a special *chrisma* along with an exclusive *gnosis* that they believed John's Christian community was not enlightened enough to understand.

> **PERSONAL RESPONSE:** Describe how it feels when someone claims a special knowledge or enlightenment that is superior to yours. Respond in the margin.

I found this piece of historical background fascinating: very possibly John was encouraging and reminding the faithful of his church by using two of the secessionist's own terms in verse 20, *chrisma* and *gnosis*.[8] If I can paraphrase John, I hear him saying to his beloved children, "The secessionists want to talk about a special anointing and knowledge? Let me tell you about the special anointing and knowledge—you already have it in Christ."

This means a lot to me right now in the Internet age where we're the recipients of limitless opinions, "new" theologies, "progressive" ideas and doctrines. We can see what spiritual niches and worldviews are trending. And it's easy to suddenly think we're missing out on some special *chrisma*—that this new group or that smart and thoughtful tribe or this pristine author have finally figured it all out. Because of "new" enlightenment we're led to believe that the orthodox truths of Scripture are antiquated or have been misinterpreted for thousands of years.

> While false anointings come and go, the *chrisma* John describes in verse 27 has an enduring quality. "The anointing you received from him _Remains_ in you."

> **PERSONAL REFLECTION:** Name one truth of the gospel or of Jesus' teaching that you consistently come back to regardless of how culture shifts.

> What does the anointing do in our lives (v. 27)?
> ❑ encourages   ❑ blesses
> ❑ comforts   ☑ teaches

Jesus speaks of the Holy Spirit's role as Teacher in John's Gospel. Look up the following passages and respond to the corresponding questions.

> Of what does the Holy Spirit also remind us according to John 14:26?
> _every thing Jesus has said_
> Jesus calls the Holy Spirit "the Spirit of _Truth_ " (John 15:26).

Today's arguments for more enlightened ways of life apart from Scripture are not all that different from what the pre-gnostics of John's day were arguing for. I've personally struggled in this sea of swirling opinions, even some from within the Christian community who are suggesting that since everyone's interpretation of the Bible is flawed, it's really impossible to know what Scripture clearly teaches on any given matter.

While the Bible is indeed full of mystery and complexities, the tenets of the Christian faith and the ways in which we've been called to live are more plain than we sometimes want to admit. I can't imagine why Jesus would send us the Holy Spirit to lead us into all truth if truth can't be known. This brings us to the next part of verse 27 where John describes one of the benefits and functions of our anointing.

> I can't imagine why Jesus would send us the Holy Spirit to lead us into all truth if truth can't be known.

PERSONAL REFLECTION: What causes you to doubt the validity of God's Word and the guidance of the Holy Spirit? Be specific, naming cultural examples or influential relationships in your life. Respond in the margin.

John says that because we have the anointing, we don't need…
- ❑ to study the Word
- ❑ anyone's help
- ☑ anyone to teach us
- ❑ to serve the poor

This verse can easily be misconstrued, so a quick word about it. We could look at a verse like this and think we don't need pastors, teachers, or spiritual mentors. As attractive as this may be for those who want to hibernate from fellowship and instruction (I've been there), it's clear from John's letters that this is not what he means. John's whole letter is full of teaching. So, again, it's important to consider the other verses around this verse as well as the context of the day.

The dissenting false teachers were telling the church members that they needed a "higher" teaching, more enlightenment to really know the truth. In light of this, John was reminding his readers that they had been anointed by the Holy One (the Teacher), and that the truth of God's Word contained, "all that [they needed] to know at any one time."[9]

I want to close today's study with an encounter that happened many years before John wrote his epistles. He had been part of anointing a man named Stephen for the work of the ministry in Acts 6:2-5. Stephen faced intense opposition and eventually was martyred. But something very interesting was said about him that directly relates to the anointing of the Spirit and His undeniable truth. Read Acts 6:8-10.

82

What were the people who opposed Stephen ultimately unable to stand up against? (v. 10)

his Wisdom + The Spirit by whom he Spoke

Notice, the passage doesn't say they couldn't stand up against Stephen's wit, Ivy League education, razor sharp intellect, wealth, experience, or resources. These are wonderful accolades but the Holy Spirit and His wisdom are superior still.

I have a friend who often laments over not being smarter, or a better debater in areas of biblical truth. She complains of not having all the informed, relevant arguments, or not being quick enough to grab a verse from here or there. But when people are in her presence they experience the power of the Spirit in her and the truth of God's Word lived out in her actions. She has a clear anointing on her life and it's more powerful than any clever argument or human reasoning.

> **PERSONAL REFLECTION:** Describe a time when the Holy Spirit through God's Word taught you something you couldn't have otherwise known. Do you need His wisdom right now? Ask Him for it.

The anointing of the Holy Spirit and the accompanying truth of God's Word can't be overstated. My prayer for you today is that you sense your anointing, your *chrisma*, in your workplace, at your dinner table, during your business trip. Jesus Himself has set you apart for a sacred purpose. In essence He's poured the consecrating oil over you, He's stroked it across your forehead, you are sealed with His Spirit.

This *chrisma* opens your eyes to what is truth and what is not. John begins verse 27 (NIV) with, "as for you." It doesn't matter what everyone else is up to. YOU abide in Him. Sometimes we have to quit looking around us and go back to the beginning, do what we know to do, let Him teach us, and dwell safely within Him. All kinds of teachings will come and go, but never abdicate the truth that remains in you. Do this by remaining in Him.

CHILDREN OF GOD

Today is one of those days where I want you to begin by simply reading the text. At first it may seem like John is all over the place, but after reading it several times I began to notice all his ideas settling into a single stream of thought, at least mostly. Remember, as a believer in Jesus you have an anointing that teaches you, which we studied yesterday. It's the perfect time to let Him lead you and guide you into the truth He promises as you study God's Word. Read 1 John 3:1-10 meditatively.

Observation 1:

I read and reread these verses several times and with each reading a new thought emerged to the surface. In the margin write two of your observations.

In verses 1 and 2, John says something twice. What does he call us?

dear Children

Observation 2:

What other words or ideas in verses 1-10 does John use that relate to being children of God?

dear Friends, dear Children

My brother David is 8 years younger than I am, the towering six-foot-three baby of the family. I still find it unbearably heartwarming and equally startling to hear his three year-old son Will call him, "Daddy." Perhaps this is because I can remember my brother holding the television hostage with Nickelodeon episodes, rattling the last ounces of milk from the milk carton, and generally getting in my superior teenage way. Today, though, he is a father. And listening to Will tell me about how his daddy smashed a spider earlier that day, his nose wrinkled and eyes on fire, proud as a peacock over his dad's prowess to conquer and protect, melts me. Your father may have been absent, or perhaps you had a good one. Even the fathers who love us are still deeply flawed. But today you can take harbor in the truth that you are a child of God. If you do nothing else today, allow that truth to have its way with you.

PERSONAL REFLECTION: In verse 1, John links our being children of God with the lavish love of the Father. How do you see the two being connected?

Turn to John's Gospel and read verses 1:10-13. Describe what it means to be born of God. Respond in the margin.

Received Christ + Believed in his name – became Children of God.

Flip back to 1 John 3. Notice the emphasis John puts on our identity as God's children in verse 2. He says that we are God's children…
- ❏ when we are born
- ❏ when we are flawless
- ❏ when we get to heaven
- ☑ now

So often I have tried to fight my own battles, rely on my own strength, drain my resources to the dregs in a full-on panic, when all the while I have a Father. The Father. What if we recognized that we are lavishly loved by Him, as a tender father bends to hold his beloved child?

PERSONAL RESPONSE: How can you allow this present reality to meet you in the circumstances you are currently facing? Respond in the margin.

Being a child of God in the present would seem to be enough, but John goes on to promise an even greater reality. Though John acknowledges we can't fully understand what we'll be like in heaven, according to verse 2, what does he promise is to come?

We Shall be Like him –

PERSONAL TAKE: Verse 3 is an interesting verse I had to ponder. How should the hope of Christ's return and the glory that follows affect your present moral purity? Just let your pen flow on this one.

When I find myself without hope it's often because I'm not dwelling enough on what's to come. When I dwell on what's to come—seeing Jesus as He is and being made like Him—it directly affects my present and the daily choices I make. John's writing about the love of the Father and the hope we have for the future is not merely for our theological understanding. Rather it's because this future reality has present implications. Our beliefs affect the way we live now. The next few verses move into these practicalities. Reread 1 John 3:4-10.

Since John tends to repeat himself at points, we're going to separate these seven verses up into two groups: the "negative" warnings of sin and the positive declarations of righteousness. In the columns that follow list everything that applies to the categories. I've filled in an example for you in each column. My personal understanding reflects the idea put forward by many scholars—that John is speaking of habitual, continual, and deliberate sin as a way of life when he speaks of "those who sin."

NEGATIVE WARNINGS	POSITIVE DECLARATIONS
You can't be born of God and sin habitually, as a way of life.	The Son of God appeared to destroy the devil's work
Continues to sin has not seen him or known him	He who does what is right is righteous
He who does what is Sinful is of the devil	
anyone who does not do what is right is not a child of God	

I wanted to break these out in columns because it's easy to get lost in John's style. Sometimes when I read him I feel like I'm on the phone with that friend who never takes a breath. John hardly pauses, one thought flowing into the next and back again like a circular stream. But as I sit with him I think I'm getting the overarching idea. I hope you are too.

PERSONAL TAKE: If you had to sum up the core message of verses 4-10 in one sentence, what would you write? There's no right answer.

We live in a culture that makes little of sin and often relabels sin as progress or something to celebrate. Even within the church people are questioning and attempting to overturn timeless moral and theological truths from God's Word. John passionately reminds us that practicing sin as a way of life is incongruent with being born of God and knowing Him. The two simply cannot go together (see vv. 6, 8).

The first sentence of verse 7 is so passionate, so vital to us in our day and age. Write John's warning here: "Dear/Little children
do not let anyone led you astray -

I used to walk to my elementary school. Down Carlsbad Ct., up Claxton, a left on Bradwell, and across the main cut-through to Fox Mill Elementary. If my Mom told me once, she told me one hundred times to beware of strangers when walking to school. She even described what they might look like, or phrases they might use to lure me. In essence, she would tell me not to be deceived and then she would give me parameters and a context for how not to be deceived—don't go off with a stranger who pulls up and wants you to get in his car. John does the same thing.

How does John tell us that we can know who is righteous and who is sinful, and therefore not to be deceived? (vv. 7-8)

Righteous - does what is right
Sinful — does what is sinful

Of course this is not a license to pin on a moral-police badge while going around writing tickets to every sinner we see. "I see you have sinned, you must be of the devil." This is not the spirit behind what John is saying, though I don't want to dilute him in any way. Remember the context of John's day: People who claimed to be followers of Jesus were not living according to His ways. An entire group in the church had packed their bags, denying the truth of Jesus. John wanted to protect his people from these secessionists.

John's way of discerning between who was truly a child of God and who was not was straightforward: You simply can't be born of God and continue a lifestyle contrary to who God is. Again, I don't believe John's warning was for the sake of crossing our arms and judging who is saved and who is not (salvation belongs to our God). Rather, in a circumstance of grave deceit and confusion, he was bringing clarity to his church: Don't be deceived by people who claim to know Christ but whose lives clearly contradict His will and way. John's congregation needed the discernment to guard against being carried off with these spiritual castaways, not so they could piously condemn others.

> **PERSONAL REFLECTION:** Read verses 3:1-10 again. While reading, ask the Holy Spirit to reveal any areas of sin you have dismissed or even relabeled as goodness. Respond in the margin.

I think the tendency is to look at a text like verses 4-10 and forget its anchor in verses 1-3. Choosing moral purity according to Scripture is not about some moral high ground the Christian is to take for the sake of self-righteousness, but rather the choice has its roots in being the very children of God. It's about living like who we are! Those born of God will do righteousness, because that is Christ's nature and we are in Christ.

So naturally the question arises, *what happens if I'm struggling in sin, does this mean I'm not truly a child of God?* I've been twirling this around in my sorely finite brain, trying to get at John's meaning. Was he being extra dogmatic because of the conditions of the day where so many had denied Jesus, yet still claimed God? Was he talking about continuous, willful, deliberate sin as a lifestyle? I'll tell you where I'm landing, but I hope you will keep studying and praying for discernment for yourself.

Those born of God will do righteousness, because that is Christ's nature and we are in Christ.

Every believer in Christ is a child of God and is born of God (1 John 3:1,9)

Based on 1 John 1:8-10, is it possible for believers to be without sin?

John has established that no one is without sin and when believers do sin we have an Advocate in Jesus who is faithful to forgive and cleanse us. So we can take *living a perfectly sinless life* off the table, while we leave *astounding forgiveness because of Jesus* on. Still, we are left with some tricky statements, one being: "Everyone who is born of God does not sin (or practice sin)." My gut reaction is to soften John here, to find a loophole, to lower the bar—*surely John couldn't demand that high a standard, could he?*

But then I started wondering what would happen if we really focused on what I think the theme is here: The ramifications of being a child of God. Perhaps then we wouldn't feel the need to tweak John's meaning— maybe a life free of sin is more possible than we thought. So let's break this down together from the text.

- Verse 3:1. BEING A CHILD OF GOD is directly connected to the Father's lavish _Love_ for us.

- Verses 3:5-6. BEING A CHILD OF GOD means He sent His Son Jesus to take away our _Sins_. And now as we live our lives we are actually living them in Christ!

- Verse: 3:8. BEING A CHILD OF GOD means His Son, Jesus, came to destroy the Devil's…

  ❏ kingdom ❏ strongholds
  ❏ schemes ☑ works (all of the above)

- Verse 3:9. BEING A CHILD OF GOD means the seed of God's Word _remains_ in us.

- Verse 3:9. BEING A CHILD OF GOD means we have been:

  ❏ called by God ☑ born of God
  ❏ raised by God ❏ loved by God

PERSONAL RESPONSE: Out of these five truths, what means the most to you as it relates to your attitude, the way you love others, what your mouth speaks, your moral behavior? Why?

I wish we had the chance to hash these verses out in person. These types of passages are almost better understood in a seeping sort of way, rather than an intellectual light bulb suddenly flicking on. If I could leave you with what my heart is currently pounding over, it's this: A life of righteousness, free of the dominant power of sin, is directly, inextricably connected to our relationship with God. We come to this text and try to figure out how much sin is too much sin. Then we try to fix things in our own flesh. But our not sinning is not about how much harder we try. It's about our relationship with our Father and His Son.

When we consider His lavish love, His Word planted in our heart by the Father, we will begin to rely on the power of Jesus to destroy the Devil's work. When we fall back on Jesus to take away our sins—all of them— realizing that we are not just someone the Lord tolerates, someone He let slip in, but that Jesus actually chose us, then maybe we will realize what John is saying really is possible: We can be free of sin.

PERSONAL RESPONSE: Finish today by considering what's holding you down. What sin has gripped you? Respond however the Lord is leading. Just know that I'm cheering you on, absolutely convinced that you and I can overcome in Jesus' name.

DAY 5
A LIFE LAID DOWN

Jesus appeared in the flesh to take away our sins and to destroy the Devil's work (1 John 3:4,8)

Today we're going to talk about love. I know, by now you're probably thinking how grossly mistitled this Bible study is with a name like, *What Love Is*. You're thinking I should have called it *What Sin Is* or *How Complicated John's Letters Are*. I have wanted to retitle this study several times already, but it's texts like today's that remind me that Jesus' love is still the loudest voice. Once again, will you settle your soul and open your heart for what God longs to bring you today? Please read 1 John 3:11-15.

I hope someone out there is even slightly like me, because when I first read verse 11, "we should love one another," I was warmed at such a lovely, simple, obtainable concept. Then I wanted to die when John went straight into Cain and Abel and how Cain murdered Abel because he was from the Evil One. Can anything be light with John? Can we have one breezy moment of love? The answer is yes and no. Hang with me. Flip to Genesis 4:1-8 just to familiarize yourself with the story.

> Why was Cain angry, per the Genesis account? Note: while the passage doesn't clearly state why Abel's offering was acceptable to the Lord, the implication is that the acceptability of a fat offering (animal sacrifice) had been made clear to both Cain and Abel.

> **PERSONAL TAKE:** What other emotions, besides anger, can you deduce Cain felt toward Abel and why? (Consider both accounts in Genesis and 1 John as you answer.) Respond in the margin.

Not all jealousy or anger leads to murder, but John shows us what could. Of course in the Sermon on the Mount Jesus calls out our heart on this matter (see Matt. 5:22-24). Though John spends a few verses discussing hate and murder, remember his point is that we're to love one another. John hasn't abandoned the positive note he began on, but he wants to make sure none of us is harboring hatred, in particular, toward a brother or sister in Christ. So let's take a moment with this—love is at stake.

The Holy Spirit may have already brought someone to mind. Someone you're jealous of, hold anger or bitterness towards, someone you haven't forgiven and still want to see repaid. Maybe it's even taking the subtler form of gossip. Perhaps you do what I sometimes do, which is hope a verse like this does not apply to that one person who walked out on you, hurt you, or betrayed you. As if harboring animosity toward just one person at a time is somehow OK. Again, my tendency is to want to pacify John here, but love is too noble and hate too devouring to tame John's words. Love is bound to Jesus' death and hate can lead to murder, so we need to come to terms with our stuff here.

> **PERSONAL REFLECTION:** Is there anyone you hate, are holding onto bitterness toward, or haven't forgiven? Do you feel jealous like Cain? Would you take some time to confess this before the Lord so you can be free to love?

> You may be experiencing the opposite problem. Someone may hate you for the same reason Cain hated Abel. First John 3:12 gives us that two-fold reason. What is it?

Cain's actions were evil
ABLe's actions were righteous

PERSONAL REFLECTION: Jesus told us not to be surprised about the disdain some will have for us as believers. Read John's Gospel 15:18-20. Are any relationships in your life strained because of your faith in Christ and your obedient lifestyle? Though Jesus' words are solemn, how can you find comfort in them?

Back to 1 John 3:16-18. Verse 16 gives a definition of what love is (how we come to know it):
Jesus Christ __*LAid*____*down*____*his*__ life for us.

We'll look at this more deeply in chapter 4, but for now, how are we to emulate this love? (v. 16)
Lay down our Lives for the brothers.

Consider what Reuben Welch says about laying your life down: "As long as I can read that verse and say I'd be willing to die if I have to, I can go my way untouched and unrebuked. But when it says to me put it down, brother—put your life down—then that meets me day by day and challenges me to decisions and discipleship."[10] The idea of laying down our lives for others is so vital to the Christian faith, I want to make sure we have a grasp of the meaning. Briefly read in John's Gospel 15:13 and 10:11-18 for further insight.

PERSONAL REFLECTION: Based on the John passages, what does laying your life down for others actually look like?

I've always considered Jesus' death on the cross as the meaning of His laying down His life for us. It never occurred to me that Jesus laid His life down for us well before the cross; "For thirty-three years Jesus laid down His life to do the will of His Father."[11] I relate to what Oswald Chambers says next, "It is much easier to die than to lay down your life day in and day out with the sense of the high calling of God."[12]

PERSONAL RESPONSE: Is there any area where you're currently holding your life back, trying to preserve your way, your wants and desires? How is God asking you to lay your life down for another? Don't be afraid to let this get uncomfortable.

Jesus is the embodiment of love who laid down His life for us (I John 3:16)

Back to 1 John 3:17-18. John gets really specific with us in these verses. (Hooray for concrete examples in 1 John!)

What practical examples does he give us?

Brother in need — you have material possessions but have no pity on him.

I appreciate what scholar I. Howard Marshall says about verse 17, "Christian love is love which gives to those in need … John is talking about a feeling of pity which expresses itself in action."[13]

PERSONAL REFLECTION: What specific situations cause you to feel compassion, heartache, or pity for people? Take note of what specifically moves you about the brokenness of the human condition. What actions can you take to show the love of Christ?

PERSONAL TAKE: John says we're to love not only in word and speech, but with actions and truth. What do you think it means to love in truth?

actions + truth.

In verse 17 John uses the most powerful phrase to describe withholding pity or compassion from people ("closing your eyes to them," HCSB). It is the Greek word *splagchnon*. It literally means your innards or intestines, the seat of the strong passions like anger and love.

PERSONAL REFLECTION: Pardon the graphic phrase, but describe the last time you felt a love so deep for someone that it seemed to come from your intestines.

Essentially, when we withhold compassion or close our eyes to the needs of others, we are shutting the core of our innards to the person. I absolutely love what Reuben Welch says about this: "When you have had your feelings hurt, where does it hurt? And when you are heavy-hearted, where does the weight rest? Not in your heart, but in your "splangknas"—that's where."[14] Though it's sometimes painful to love this wholly, I'm always grateful when the Lord helps me love as deep as my *splangknas*. I need to pray that God would give me more of this. I think it's a prayer He delights in answering because that kind of love is the very love of God.

When we withhold ourselves from people who need us, John asks the question "How can the love of God abide in you?" Welch goes onto say, "Does that say anything to us about the way God loves? It says to us that God has opened up his insides to us."[15]

I'm not capable of loving the way I long to love. I'm not capable of laying my life down for others the way Jesus has asked me to. But when I understand loving that fully is actually the love of God in me, well, that's another story.

> **PERSONAL RESPONSE OPTION 1:** You may be in a place where the Lord is calling you to lay your life down for another in a specific instance. If this is you—even if it seems like the most insignificant of ways—respond to God about what He's asking of you.

> **PERSONAL RESPONSE OPTION 2:** You may need a deeper understanding of the love that God poured out on you. You'll never love others if you haven't first grasped His love. Spend some time asking the Lord to open your eyes to the way He's poured His love out for you.

What else can I say but that we're halfway there? After the somewhat stark warnings from earlier in chapter 3, today's verses should have felt like gentle winds of encouragement. I hope you received them that way. As we end this most powerful chapter, how glorious the reminder that we are born of God. How empowering to realize we have been set apart with an anointing from Jesus Himself, that stunning *chrisma*. We don't have to be bound up in jealousy and hate like Cain, instead we are free to lay our lives down for one another. And this comes with great reward.

As we close our week about love, may we never forget its definition in Jesus: "The word love needs a dictionary and for Christians the dictionary is Jesus Christ. He took that chameleon of a word and gave it a fast color so that ever since it has lustered with his life and teaching—dyed in the crimson of Calvary and shot through with the glories of Easter morning."[16] Amen and amen.

BIG FAT GREEK SALAD

FROM THE KITCHEN OF KELLY MINTER

I'm always looking for dishes that are easy and fresh but with a hint of something different. This salad is that dish. The hearts of palm, artichoke hearts, sundried tomatoes, and special dressing give this salad a nice flair. I know that cooking isn't primarily supposed to be about impressing people, but if you need to impress, this is a good oh-it-was-nothing type salad.

INSTRUCTIONS

In a large ziplock bag marinate 2 boneless, skinless chicken breasts in the marinade and refrigerate for 30 min. to 1 hour. While the chicken marinates, mix together your greek salad dressing and chop ingredients for your salad. Put your lettuce in a large salad bowl and then arrange other salad ingredients on top.

Grill chicken for 25-30 minutes or until done on an outdoor grill. Slice chicken into strips. Toss salad with greek dressing and then serve with chicken.

CHICKEN MARINADE

- 2 Tablespoons olive oil
- 1 handful of fresh chopped oregano (can substitute dried if you need to)
- Juice from 1 whole lemon
- Salt and pepper
- 1/4 cup water

GREEK SALAD DRESSING

- 4 Tablespoons Olive Oil
- Juice from one whole lemon (add more lemon juice to make it zestier)
- 2 Tablespoons water
- Greek seasoning like from Zoe's Kitchen to taste (or substitute mixture of dried oregano, dried basil, salt, pepper, garlic powder, and dried rosemary)
- Fresh ground pepper
- Whisk together and set aside

SALAD INGREDIENTS:

- Chopped romaine lettuce or mixed greens
- Chopped hearts of palm
- Chopped artichoke hearts
- Chopped sundried tomatoes
- Feta Cheese
- Optional: toasted pine nuts

Optional: serve with warm pita bread and tzatziki sauce!

CHRISTMAS FRENCH TOAST
FROM THE KITCHEN OF MEGAN MINTER

My mom used to serve this dish to our family every Christmas morning and now my sister prepares it. I thought it would be a fun meal for any groups who meet in the morning.

RECIPE INGREDIENT LIST

- 1 cup brown sugar
- 1/2 cup melted butter
- 3 tsp cinnamon
- 3 tart apples, peeled and sliced (I use Granny Smith)
- 1/2 cup dried cranberries
- 1 loaf of French bread, sliced
- 6 large eggs
- 1 1/2 cup milk
- 1 Tbs vanilla

INSTRUCTIONS

Combine brown sugar and butter and 1 tsp. cinnamon. Add apples and cranberries. Toss to coast. Spread apples over bottom of baking dish. Arrange slices of bread on top. (They can be sliced 1/2 inch or slightly bigger). Mix eggs, milk, vanilla and 2 tsp cinnamon. Pour over bread. Cover and refrigerate 4-24 hours. (We put it together on Christmas Eve!) Bake covered with aluminum foil at 375 degrees for 45 minutes. Uncovered and bake 5 more minutes. 12 servings.

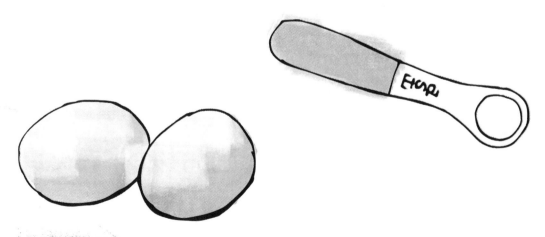

EASTER EVERYDAY

My niece and nephew were over for an Easter egg hunt at my house. It was a balmy 70 degrees, ocean blue skies, and if I do say so myself, my lawn was in lush form. My sister was in town and we'd meticulously hidden the eggs for our three-year old nephew, Will, and our one-and-a-half-year-old niece, Harper. Might I mention that romaine lettuce is the perfect garden vegetable in which to hide an Easter egg? I'm doing this every year until they're thirty. I don't even care. The egg nestles perfectly between the leaves, like the stigma of a flower between its petals. And kids think it's the funniest thing they've ever seen. Like, hilarious. Will could barely go on for laughing so hard at the incongruity of it all—an Easter egg in the lettuce? Stop it.

While Will was busy opening eggs and depleting them of their jellybeans, Harper was spotting eggs, picking them up, giving them a thorough look over and then putting them back down. She had no idea the blessing of candy that hid in the center. *Such a neat activity this is, dressing up and finding brightly colored plastic eggs in the yard for no good reason,* is how I think she was looking at all this.

Meanwhile, one of my best friends called in an Easter-morning panic. We'd just celebrated the Risen Savior at church with a string section, exuberant worship, and a poignant sermon. I couldn't imagine what could have already gone wrong.

"Some animal has gotten into all my Easter eggs!" This is where planning ahead by hiding all your eggs the night before can come back to bite you. I'm now an even bigger fan of procrastination.

"What are you talking about?"

"A hawk got into them and so did the squirrels." She ranted. "Candy and wrappers are all over my yard. I'm going to have to pull out a gun on Easter."

I found this to be a problem on so many levels. Not the least of which is that if ever a squirrel should be exonerated for tearing into a Reese's Peanut Butter Cup, I feel it should be on Easter. Now a hawk I just have no sympathies for, but a squirrel? Not to mention I just didn't think the Lord could be pleased with the use of a BB gun on Easter Sunday.

I thought my friend might be exaggerating but by the time I got over there she had a trove of evidence. Plastic eggs that had been ripped into with abandon, wrappers all over the yard, chocolate chunks with teeth marks on them. I'm not even sure how these creatures managed; it was actually kind of impressive. Thankfully she had extra candy and eggs and was able to get everything sorted out by the time eight dear children arrived for their hunt. The day was saved.

The glory of the afternoon reminded me that while Christmas has always held top billing in my heart, Easter is gaining on Christmas' heels. I think this is because the older I get the more I'm aware of my sin—not just the sins a person commits in a day—but my sin. The selfish and critical thoughts that lurk in my heart. The inability to grab love out of my flesh for people who have hurt me, betrayed me, or who simply drive me nutso. The daily reality that I need a Savior. The awareness that there really is no good thing that dwells in my heart apart from Christ, even though He created me wonderfully and beautifully and loves me more than I can imagine.

So Easter is hitting me bigger and brighter with every year as I really drink in what Jesus has done for me. How He's taken my sin upon Himself even though He knew no sin. And not just the sin of the world but all my specific "stuff"; the stuff I know and He knows and a few believers I get to confess to for the sake of freedom and healing know.

This week we'll look at some of the elements that make Easter so unfathomable, so sobering, and so downright celebratory. We'll examine the amazing truths of Jesus, His incarnation, His death, and the atonement He has made for us. Truths I know John rejoiced in all year long.

My prayer is that as we look at these truths we'll crack open their shells for what's inside. In Bible study it's too easy to go through the motions, fill in the blanks but never allow the truths to penetrate our hearts. To put on the dress, find the egg and put it right back down where we found it, never getting to the treasure inside. We also have a tendency to allow distractions, lies, and unbelief to pluck those truths out of our hearts. It's the way Jesus described a farmer tossing seed into the ground only for that seed to be choked by the cares of the world or plucked by the birds of the air (or by hawks and squirrels looking for Peeps®).

As we look at familiar tenets of the gospel this week, I encourage you to get inside them. An intellectual understanding or a correct answer is not really the goal. Take it all in. Ask the Holy Spirit to help you get at the core of the Word and the Word to get at the core of you. Don't let the familiarity of certain verses or ideas dull you into missing resurrection truths. The Scriptures were meant to point us to Jesus, the One who changes lives and brings new life. Easter truths await us.

VIEWER GUIDE

KNOWLEDGE AND ASSURANCE

Affirmation #1 What we believe about _____.

Affirmation #2 That we obey His _____.

Affirmation #3 The way we love _____.

Affirmation #4 Other _____ affirm Jesus in us.

Affirmation #5 The _____ _____.

GROUP DISCUSSION QUESTIONS:

What was the most impacting moment for you this week (in video or print study)?

Which of the five affirmations from the video gives you the greatest sense of assurance?

Have you fretted over whether or not you really know God? How did today's teaching give you more confidence? In what areas are you still unsettled?

How does the pre-gnosticism that had infiltrated the church of John's day remind you of similar deceptions in current culture?

What most encourages you about the anointing you have from the Holy Spirit? What challenges you most about it? (p. 75)

GOD IS GREATER

We've heard the phrase, "I'm my own worst enemy." When you give this any thought it seems a ridiculous notion, that we would soldier up against ourselves. But how often we do just that; our minds whisper that we'll never be a kinder mom, or the woman a desirable man would want to marry, or the warrior-type who could have conquered that deplorable habit. Sometimes we even tell ourselves that we're dirty, unloved, rejected. John understood—our hearts have a tendency to condemn us. I think you'll find today both intriguing and relieving. Read 1 John 3:19-24.

Keep in mind that when John begins with "this is how we know," he's likely referring back—we can know what he's about to tell us in verses 19-24 based on verses 10-18. Let's begin with verses 19-20. Because this is a difficult passage to layout grammatically, and translations do it differently, refer to the following version for consistency:

> *"And by this we will know that we are of the truth, and we will set our hearts at ease before him, whenever our hearts condemn us, for God is greater than our hearts and knows all things."[1]*

PERSONAL TAKE: Look back at verses 16-18 from last week. How do you think living out these principles affirm verse 19—that we're living in the truth?

PERSONAL REFLECTION: Think about the last time you loved someone by doing something for him (action) that was rooted in the knowledge of the gospel (truth). Did that experience help assure you that you belonged to the truth (or "belonged to God," is another safe translation)? Describe it if you can point to anything concrete.

If you can't pinpoint anything yet, don't worry. I'm still getting my head around this one as well. The clearest example I thought of was when helping an impoverished family get ready for church, both parents with physical ailments crammed into an exceedingly small apartment with their four children. The youngest child had broken his leg. The mother was trying to change his diaper despite the awkward cast and her disability. The other kids were racing around in their hand-me-down clothes, readying themselves for Wednesday night church. The whole scene bowled me over and the minute I dropped them off in the church parking lot I sobbed. I knew God had given me a love for them that was leading to action—this helped me know I belonged to God.

> Not only does loving others help assure us we belong to the truth, John mentions another benefit in verse 19. What is it?

PERSONAL REFLECTION: Does your heart ever condemn you (even rightly so)? Do you avoid God's presence because you're riddled with guilt, shame, or a sense you don't measure up? How does this affect your relationship with the Lord?

Set our hearts at rest in his presence

The Greek word for being at rest in His presence is *peisomen,* and can mean: *reassure, pacify, conciliate, set at ease.*[2] I absolutely love this imagery, especially up against a condemning heart—which means *to blame or find fault with*. As one who has often felt saddled with guilt, always trying to do better, I am drawn to this picture of settledness in God's presence. I picture a fearful or anxious child, maybe even feeling guilty because he's gotten into something he shouldn't have. Then comes the calming voice of the parent, the tender thumbs that wipe away the tears, the pats on the back, the nestling close that relieves the angst. I sense the child's punctuated gasps turn from crying to measured breathing. He's now at ease in his father's arms, the one who's greater and stronger than anything the child has feared.

When I think of God being greater than my heart because He "knows all things," that frankly doesn't give me a whole lot of comfort. I take that to mean that He knows more about my dark heart than even I do. But enjoy this quote by Robert W. Yarbrough: John's writing "is to remind readers that in coming before God, they approach one who knows everything about all hearts, yet is still able to forgive."[3]

While thinking about verse 19, I remembered one of my favorite verses from the Psalms. I wonder if John, who would have been very familiar with the Psalms, had Psalm 103:13-14 in mind? (See the margin.)

As a father has compassion on his children, so the LORD has compassion on those who fear him. For he knows how we are formed, he remembers that we are dust.

Psalm 103:13-14

How do you think God's knowledge of who we are plays into His compassion toward us?

If I had to guess, I think John is assuring his church in two ways: One, he says they love in action and in truth. Their tangible care for the body of Christ is a fruit of who they are in Jesus. Two, God knows everything about us, He knows us better than our hearts do, and still "the love and mercy of the Father are present to heal [our] troubled consciences."[4]

Since the ideas behind 1 John 3:21-22 are similar to 5:14-15, I'll address prayer and confidence before God when we get to that chapter. Keep the flow of those verses in mind, but for now let's move on to verse 23.

In verse 23, what is God's two-part command?
Part One: Believe in the _Name_ of Jesus Christ
Part Two: _Love_ one another

LET'S ADDRESS PART 1. This is the first time John has explicitly mentioned belief in Jesus, and he says we're to believe in His name.

PERSONAL TAKE: What does Jesus' name represent to you?

At the time of John's writing, much like today, many false beliefs were circulating about who Jesus was. We've talked about the gnostics who denied certain attributes of His being and divinity. To believe in Jesus' name was to believe everything He claimed about Himself and His teachings, and to put one's trust in His being. It wasn't a fickle belief or a merely intellectual belief that we see so much in our culture. I have acquaintances who generally live however they want, tacking "but, I love Jesus" onto whatever they're doing. But to believe in Jesus' name is to submit ourselves to Him, to go where He goes, agree with His ways, enjoy His fellowship. It's to have all of Him.

LET'S ADDRESS PART 2. Let's visit the second half of the command. We're to love one another. This is an important time to define our terms because our English Bibles use a single word *love* to represent a few Greek words that are actually quite different in meaning. The two main Greek words for *love* used in 1, 2, and 3 John (and John's Gospel) are *agapao* and *agape*.[5] I've also included *phileo* for comparison. Please take a moment to read the definitions for the three terms. They appear in the margin.

We'll come back to these definitions, but for now, note that both *agapao* and *agape* are love born out of choice and will. We may not always feel this kind of love like we do with *phileo*, but they are powerful forms of love, nonetheless. After John's consecutive mentions that we're to love one another—with more coming—I finally had to ponder, *do I love these people? Do I really love them the way Jesus is talking about?*

> **PERSONAL RESPONSE:** Has the Holy Spirit brought a person to mind to whom you're not showing love? How can you take an action step of love in obedience to His command in verse 23?

If we put part 1 and part 2 of verse 23 together, here's the reality: We can't separate loving others from our belief in Jesus. Both are intertwined. Our confession of Him will lead to action, and true love in action will result from our knowing Him. Belief without love can make you a Pharisee. Love without belief can make you a humanitarian. But if you have both, you're a child of God.

We'll finish today with verse 24, the final verse of chapter 3. And a beautiful one it is. Please read verse 24 again.

> The one who obeys His commands…
> ☑ lives/remains in God
> ❑ has God living/remaining in Him
> ❑ both
>
> We're back to that Greek word *meno* from Week 3 Day 2. Write as much about that word from memory as you can. (Feel free to look back for help.)

Last week we received a much fuller picture of this word when we looked at the branch remaining in the vine in John 15. We looked at verses 1-8, but today I want to look further at verses 9-10. Please turn to John's Gospel and read verses 15:9-10.

Agapao: "to love, indicates a direction of the will and finding one's joy in something. *Agapao* is used of God's love toward man and vice versa."

Agape: is a "benevolent love. Its benevolence, however, is not shown by doing what the person loved desires but what the one who loves deems as needed by the one loved. God's love for man is His doing what He thinks best for man and not what man desires."

Phileo: "to love, with the meaning of having common interests with another."[6]

What is inextricably connected to remaining in Jesus' love?

OBEY my Commands

PERSONAL TAKE: Why do you think obeying God's commands is synonymous with loving Him? Explain.

PERSONAL REFLECTION: Jesus told the disciples in verse 9 that He already loved them. How does this reality help you better understand what it means to remain in His love? In other words, if He already loves us, remaining in His love must be something different than trying to earn His love. Journal your thoughts.

Now turn to 1 John 2:3, a verse we've already studied. What else is inextricably connected to obeying His commands?

We Know...

Now back to 1 John 3:24. We can't miss that everything hinges on our obedience to God's commands, or our keeping of them, as some translations put it.

Again, this doesn't mean that we live in a paranoid state, trying to earn a place of dwelling in Christ by obeying Him—that's the opposite of what it means to dwell, right? But it does mean that abiding in Him goes hand in hand with being about what He's about, doing what He asks, caring for what He cares for.

The way I understand it is this: Obedience to Him is the outflow of our remaining in Him, and remaining in Him pours out of our obedience to Him. It's still a bit of a mystery to me but we don't have to fully understand it to experience it. If you're striving, set your heart at ease in His presence because you have an Advocate before the Father. If you want to experience His rest, choose obedience. It all leads to remaining in Him, and He in you.

TEST THE SPIRITS

PERSONAL REFLECTION: In the margin describe a conversation with someone that left you thinking, *now that you mention it, the Bible does seem a little outdated on this one.* It may have been a subtle feeling you had or it could have spun you into a doubting tailspin.

On a scale of 1-10, how persuasive was the person with whom you had the discussion? Did you feel outwitted or out-debated?

1   2   3   4   5   6   7   8   9   10

As you immerse yourself in chapter 4, keep the context of John's day in mind. Remember the antichrists? The false prophets? Those trying to lead John's beloved people astray? John is rallying his church to be discerning. Reminding them that enthusiasm, passion, or eloquence doesn't necessarily mean truth. Read 1 John 4:1-3 slowly.

Don't miss the way John addresses his readers, the way he would address us as well. "Dear Friends." Note also the term *every spirit* here applies to either "'utterance inspired by a spirit' or 'person inspired by a spirit.'"[7]

TRUE/FALSE. According to this passage only Christians claim to have spiritual inspiration.

We can recognize when a person is speaking from the spirit of God when he/she:
- ❏ has the best arguments
- ❏ is sympathetic and compassionate
- ❏ is particularly persuasive
- ❏ has a PhD
- ☑ acknowledges Jesus and His coming in the flesh
- ❏ can be backed up by science and statistics

I'm attracted to smart people. I find smart people fascinating. This is actually troubling since opposites attract. Any kind of doctor who sees me coming should sprint for the door because I will riddle him with questions. If you're a chef, forget it, don't even say hello to me. If you garden, run for your safety. Though knowledge is a gift, it's not the final authority on matters of God or truth. This doesn't mean that God doesn't love knowledge—He created it—but it's not the last word.

> If a false teacher was looking to deceive you, what characteristic or approach would have the greatest pull on you? Check from the list below, and jot the reason why next to your choice.
>
> ❑ charismatic personality   ❑ scientific evidence
> ❑ persuasive argument   ❑ compassionate heart
> ❑ eloquent delivery   ❑ other _____
>
> What does John tell us not to do with the spirits we encounter?
>
> What does he tell us to do? __*Test*__ the spirits to determine if they are from God.

The Greek word is *dokimazo* and means *to examine, to scrutinize closely.* Notice it doesn't mean condemn to hell, judge with anger, or have reason to fear. Still, the word holds weight. John implores us not to believe every thought, idea, worldview without first passing it through some sort of grid.

> What test does John give us in verse 2 that will help us recognize the Spirit of God?
>
> *Believe that Jesus Christ has come in the flesh*

Believing that Jesus Christ has come in the flesh seems like a pretty broad litmus test for whether a spirit is of God or not. We're all aware of people who don't claim to follow Christ but who nonetheless casually believe that a man named Jesus lived. They may even believe He was God's Son—the demons believe this. So what does John mean here?

> **PERSONAL TAKE:** Based on 1 John 1:6-7; 2:9-11; 3:10 how can you tell that John is talking about more than a merely casual or intellectual belief in Jesus?
>
> *fellowship + Blood of Jesus purifies us*
> *Love of the brethren.*
> *Do right + Love the brethren*

Also, from a historical standpoint, don't forget the new winds of unbelief in John's day. Some of the deceivers had a low view of Christ and others had a high view. In simplest terms, the false teachers who had a low Christological view believed that Jesus was a man and not divine, while those with a high view believed the Messiah was divine but would have never sullied Himself with a human body.

John is testifying that a true spirit of God will embrace the reality that Jesus came as both fully God and fully human. Jesus changed everything when He came to earth as the Son of God. We either accept all of Him or none of Him. The low view of Christ and the high view were the false beliefs of John's day, but today we're surrounded by countless others. Ultimately we need to be alert to any misrepresentation of Christ.[8]

> **PERSONAL REFLECTION:** Each of the following statements represent a false belief about Jesus. Finish the following sentences—you may finish them in a different way than someone else does.
>
> 1. Jesus was a good man but He's not the only …
>
> 2. It doesn't matter if you believe in Jesus, just try to …
>
> 3. I think Jesus was a good teacher, but not …
>
> 4. I believe a man named Jesus definitely lived but I don't think He should have any say over …

John says only a true spirit from God will believe Jesus came in the flesh. This is vital to our faith because, "The incarnation was not a temporary event but the permanent union of God and man in Jesus Christ."[9] Bottom line, we can recognize that a spirit is from God when that spirit honors Christ in His entirety, acknowledging all He is and claims to be. We can recognize that a spirit is not from God if that spirit denies who He is.

Read 1 John 4:4-6.

> **PERSONAL REFLECTION:** Here we get another look at the word *overcome* (remember 2:13-14). This is my favorite for so many reasons. But before I tell you why I love this word, describe a time when the Lord helped you overcome something—specifically as it relates to a false spirit or lie of the Enemy that had gotten a foothold in your life.

> According to verse 4:4, why are you able to overcome? And what does Jesus say He's already done? (See John 16:33.)
>
> *Because of the Christ in you —*

I'm feeling the need for you to be at my dining room table right now, or me at yours—depending on whether you're cooking for me. I'd like to be with you while sharing a personal story, so imagine we're together.

I used to fight anger, dating all the way back to my childhood. While legitimate reasons contributed to my anger, much of it stemmed from me not getting what I wanted when I wanted it. Or when something happened that was out of my control or that wasn't right or fair. I can still get really bent out of shape about this last one. Over time the Lord revealed to me what was causing my anger. He brought me healing through people wiser than me in the faith, through prayer and by claiming the truths of Scripture. Ultimately I can tell you the victory came because of Jesus in me, the One who's greater than everything that has the potential to make me angry. While I'm sure this could be a place of weakness for me, I really don't even think about being angry anymore. (Unless maybe I've been placed on hold by an automated service while trying to reconcile a bill.) Truly, the Lord has given me peace for anger. This is one example of how He has helped me overcome.

PERSONAL RESPONSE: You may feel discouraged over a sin or defeat. Perhaps you've succumbed to a lie that's absolutely not from God. If you've given up or are about to, meditate on the following verses about the power of Christ in you. Even read them out loud to yourself. Don't give up; you have the power of Christ to overcome.

Romans 8:11—Finish this sentence: Since the spirit who raised Jesus from the dead also dwells in me, I have the power to overcome…

Ephesians 1:18-20—Focus on one truth in these verses and describe how you can implement it into your battle to overcome.

God who is in us is greater than the Enemy who is in the world (1 John 4:4)

What specific verb is listed three times in I John 4:5-6?

Listen

Our ears are constantly taking in noise. But listening is an entirely different matter. What John is talking about is to "hear effectually … perform or grant what is spoken; to obey."[10] That the world listens to itself shouldn't surprise us. The world is committed to its pleasures, desires, and beliefs. It will seek out and listen to its own teachers. Children of God must listen to the spirit of God.

This doesn't mean we can only read expressly Christian articles, listen to Christian health advice, shop at Christian grocery stores buying Christian peaches. We live in the world and we're to love those in the world, but we should never lose our discernment. I already mentioned how much

I enjoy learning from knowledgeable people, but if in my learning (or entertainment) I find myself being drawn away from the truth of Jesus, it's imperative I stop listening to that spirit because it's not of God.

PERSONAL RESPONSE PART 1: In John 10:27 Jesus says that His sheep listen to His voice. How are you deliberately, purposefully listening to the Lord right now?

PERSONAL RESPONSE PART 2: Who or what are you listening to that you sense is drawing you away from God's truth? What deliberate, purposeful step can you take to change this?

PERSONAL TAKE: First John 4:4-6 talks about the difference between those of the world and those of God. Turn to John's Gospel, 8:23 and 17:13-19. What do you think is the difference between being in the world and being of the world?

PERSONAL REFLECTION: Describe a situation in the last month where you distinctly felt different from the world and its desires—where you realized how not-of-this-world you really are.

I want to say a special word about verse 6. If you have ever been hurt or abused by the authority of the church, verse 6 may strike terror in your heart: "We are from God, and whoever knows God listens to us; but whoever is not from God does not listen to us." Perhaps you've had a spiritual leader indicate that his or her ways were God's ways and anyone who disagreed was clearly not from God. Please remember that John wrote from a place of special privilege. He had walked with Jesus and had been given an apostolic authority that allowed him to speak so definitively. Also keep in mind the division that was discussed in 1 John 2:19. John was still in the middle of helping his readers discern what was true and what was false. So don't hear manipulative overtones in John's words. Hear the pleas of a loving church father who says, listen to me, I walked with the Savior—He's God. He came in the flesh to redeem. I love you; don't let anyone deceive you—you really are from God. Your life in this world will show it because you're in, not of it.

THIS IS LOVE

Love is an enormously broad word in our current culture, a sweeping ocean of a word that if not defined can encompass just about anything we want it to. I've had friends tell me, "it shouldn't matter what you believe just as long as you love people." Others say, "religion divides but love brings people together; can't we all just love each other and get along?" This appears reasonable until you realize that everyone has a different opinion of what love is.

Love absolutely has to be more than tolerance and it can't be less than justice, and from there we have a million competing ideas. Which is why I love John so much. Today he's going to point us to the ultimate definition of *love*, the embodiment of it, the fulfillment of this glorious word we can only begin to understand if we've first defined it.

Read 1 John 4:7-14.

Because my only good metaphors are food related, today's text is richer than triple layer chocolate ganache with fudge icing draped in sprinkles. You can't inhale this in one bite so we're going to take it a piece at a time.

In hopes of getting our heads around this passage, see the four headings below. Under each heading write in bullet point form everything John says in the passage regarding that "person."

God	the Son	those Who Know God	those Who Don't Know God
Love Comes from / Born of God / Showed his Love by sending his Son. / God Lives in us / given us his Spirit	Sent into the world we might live thru him. / atoning Sacrifice for our sins / Sent to be The Savior of the world.	Love one another / God Lives in us – his love made Complete in us – Live in him	who does not Love

PERSONAL TAKE: What stood out to you? Explain in the margin.

Here's what stood out to me: God showed His love to us by sending His Son (v. 9). I tend to focus on the love of Jesus and His sacrifice for me, but hear Spurgeon's thoughts: "Did you ever consider the depth of love in the heart of Jehovah, when God the Father equipped His Son for the great enterprise of mercy? If not, make this your day's meditation. The Father sent Him!"[11] Sometimes it's easier to relate more closely to the heart of Jesus but I never want to forget the deep love that God our Father has for you and me in sending His Son.

One of my friends mentioned how sometimes she doesn't get around to loving through a specific action because she's waiting for everything to be "just so"—you know, for the temperature to be right and the house to be cleaned and the perfect meal to be simmering in the crockpot. Others love the idea of love until someone hard to love appears. We have great intentions until the beauty of our spouse fades, a friend becomes embittered, a cranky relative moves to town. And of course there are the coworkers, in-laws, neighbors who just test us beyond our limits. We've all had moments when we realize, unequivocally, that we don't have the love it takes. This is why we must grasp verse 7.

> From where does love come?

I know of only one farm in Tennessee that sells non-homogenized, un-pasteurized milk from Jersey Cows. If I want that milk I have to buy from that farm. Similarly—except not really at all—we have to reach outside of ourselves to our only source of love. It does not come from within us. This doesn't mean we won't experience natural human affection for one another, but the higher plane, the selfless, die-to-yourself kind of love that is patient, kind, and reaches to the undeserving can only be accessed from God. He is the source of all love.

God is love and love comes from God (1 John 4:7-8)

PERSONAL RESPONSE: PART 1 Who are you having a hard time loving right now? If you don't feel safe to mention the person on paper, make up a name or nickname _____.

PERSONAL RESPONSE: PART 2 Take a moment to ask God to give you the love that comes from Him so you can give it away. He's love's eternal supply.

I can't help but notice that right in the middle of all these verses about loving God and loving others is the gospel spelled out. In a world that has a zillion ideas about what love is, John says this. is. what. it. is.

> Look back at verse 10. Let's break this down: First off, what is love not? And what does this say about God's zealous pursuit of us?

> You may have noticed in verse 10 the now familiar word *propitiation* or *atonement.* How does the meaning of this word deepen your understanding of God's love for you? (See Week 2, Day 1 if you need to refresh your memory.)

These verses contain at least ten enormous ideas, any one of which we could spend an entire lesson on. My hope is that if something grabs your heart or attention you will follow that trail as far as it takes you. Scamper off and explore. The study will be here when you return.

> Handwrite verse 11 in the margin.

We looked at this concept last week in 3:16-18, but we can't hear the command to love people enough. Why? Because we're so good at complicating the gospel. We've got theologies, denominations, agendas, prejudices, and busyness, but when these constructs obscure or block our mandate to love, we've gotten something way confused.

Flip over to Jesus' words in Matthew 22:37-40.

> Why do you think Jesus said that everything written in the Old Testament Law and everything the prophets ever taught all hangs on the command to love God and love others? Take some time to ponder and explain your thoughts.

> **PERSONAL TAKE:** Back to 1 John, I'd love your take on an interesting statement in 4:12. What do you think John means "if we love one another … his love is made complete [or perfected] in us"? And what do you think this has to do with the phrase "No one has ever seen God"?

God Is Seen In those who Love
because God Lives in Them

Last night I was at a baby shower for a dear friend who's adopting a child. My friend's love for her new daughter is part of the completion of God's love in my friend because God's love was never meant to stay holed up inside us. We doubled over with laughter delicately balanced with tears of gratitude, celebrating the homecoming of an orphan in Jesus' name; I suppose you could say I saw God. I saw Him in the invisible way John cites. Because God lives in me and in the lives of those in the room, love was present—hard, sacrificing, lay-your-life down kind of love for an orphan—I could see Him, even though no one ever has.

Just as God's love flowed through His Son and then to us, so that love is to continue to flow from us to others. When we love others, the love of God is made whole in us because it is having its full work. I think this is a little of what verse 12 means.

We'll finish with 1 John 4:13-14, two amazing verses on assurance.

How can we know that we dwell in God and He in us? (See v. 13.)

he has given us His Spirit —

PERSONAL REFLECTION: Turn to John's Gospel and read: John 14:16-17,25-26; 16:12-15. In the margin list three concrete ways the Holy Spirit brings assurance of our relationship to God.

The Holy Spirit is a Spirit of truth and also a

❑ king   ❑ friend
☑ counselor   ❑ guard

We'll talk more at the end of this week about how the Holy Spirit gives us assurance that we're in Christ. In the meantime, rest in God's specific definition of love as demonstrated through Jesus. Sometimes love means sticking it out with a person and other times it means taking a break. Some days it means hanging on for dear life and other days it means release. Love can take the form of an encouraging word or a fiery confrontation. It can mean unmerited mercy or tough lines in the sand. It can look like adopting a child or sending one out the door to fly with his own wings. It can mean staying in the most painful marriage and in some cases being forced to let one go. Love can mean giving up a career for your family and it can mean asking your family to sacrifice for the sake of your calling. But it will never go against God's laws. Love will never face-off with His promises or His design. It won't go against His Word or the quality of who He is. Love will never mean knocking Jesus' ways around, because He is love.

A LOVE THAT CASTS OUT FEAR

Fear. It captures us under a blanket of dread. Then it winds us into a frenzy or paralyzes us stiff. It asks the question, "what if …?," then abandons us to fill in the blank with the most terrifying scenarios. Fear offers no rest, no pillow for the worrier's head. Of peace, it knows nothing. Assurance is the advocate it refuses to befriend. Fear keeps us from doing what we want because *what if …?* It tells us that we can't be who God created us to be because *what if …?* Fear binds, hems, and terrifies. And perfect love kicks it out the door.

I couldn't be more hopeful about today's passage. As one who was plagued with fear, I wrap both arms around our passage today, holding it close to my chest as I am held. My prayer is that you will delight in the assuring words of John—words rooted in the love of God and the Son He sent so that we no longer have to fear.

Read 1 John 4:15-21.

> We're back to that rich word *remain/abide/dwell/live,* or *meno* in the Greek. Briefly describe its meaning. (See Week 3, Day 2 if needed) *P. 14*
>
> *Not to depart*
> *to Stay —*
>
> What is the condition for mutually abiding in God (v. 15)?
>
> *Acknowledge Jesus is the Son of God.*

Did you notice how little personal accomplishment that word *confess* or *acknowledge* conveys? We continually go to our performance, asking if we're good enough for God to love. He wants to take us as far as possible from that idea. "Whoever confesses … Jesus" (HCSB) not "who lives up to His standard." Not "who performs." Not "who doesn't sin."

Again, John begins with the point of our belief. As you'll recall, to acknowledge Jesus as the Son of God or Messiah, is to embrace all of who He says He is. This is to trust Him as nothing less than our Savior. One of the reasons John continually circles back to Jesus and His identity is because what we believe—or don't believe—about Him affects everything about the way we live our lives. What we believe matters.

PERSONAL REFLECTION: Think of one life-changing choice you've made since becoming a believer in Jesus. How did knowing Jesus affect that decision? Respond in the margin.

We need to address verses 15 and 16 together because the thoughts are intertwined. We've studied the significant Johannine theme of dwelling in God and God in us. But here in verse 16 we see something additional: "we have come to know and believe the love God has for us" (HCSB).

I want you to focus on those words *believe* and *know.* If I could live my life from the overflow of fully knowing and believing the love God has for me, I can only imagine how different my life would be. How many more people would I reach out to? What insecurities would fall by the wayside? Who would I have the courage to befriend? How much more would I want to run to Him in a moment of heartbreak? What would I be honored to set aside for His sake?

Turn to John's Gospel 6:66-69. How do Peter's words to Jesus reflect the words in 1 John 4:16? *Believe + Know -*
Know + rely

PERSONAL TAKE: Read John 18:15-17,25-27. How could Peter have claimed to know and believe in Jesus and later deny Him? How do you see this juxtaposition in your own life? Respond in the margin.
denied him ...

God's love for us, the very fact that He is love and the reality that we dwell in Him and He in us, gives us reason for confidence. John has already used the word *confidence* twice (2:28 and 3:21), but we haven't spent much time on it. The Greek word is *parresia* and is usually translated *confidence, assurance, courage,* or *boldness.* Here John connects having this kind of confidence with a specific day.

What day is it? (See 1 John 4:17.)
day of judgment

This event would have been a very familiar concept to the readers of John's day. Oddly, this is not something we hear much about today even in a relatively Christian society. I haven't seen "Day of Judgment Series, Bring A Friend" on any church placards recently. And if I did I probably wouldn't want to rush right in. Still, justice in a world that has gone woefully wrong is necessary, as much as we may recoil from the idea.

Briefly look at verses 12:47-48 in John's Gospel. Who will be judged on the day of judgment?
ones who reject Jesus + does not accept
his words.

Back to our text in 1 John, what reason does John give for why we can have confidence, of all things, on this sobering day?

- ❑ We are sinless.
- ❑ We are innocent.
- ☑ We are like Him.
- ❑ We are enlightened.

This is a tricky one at first glance because if my confidence on judgment day is directly related to how much I'm like Jesus, I have cause for concern. Don't get me wrong, holiness is my goal, but you understand. While this phrase has a few nuances, I think John Stott gets right to the heart of it when he says, "To be sure, we are not like him in our character or in our bodies … but in our standing before God, even while remaining in this world, we are already like him."[12] Because of Jesus' sacrifice for us (4:10), we are forgiven and blameless in Him before God.

Interestingly, John, who also wrote the book of Revelation, addresses this in chapter 19 verses 1-8 of that book. He talks about God's judgment of the wicked but also the purity of the bride. "Fine linen, bright and clean was given her to wear" (v. 8). Being clothed in Christ's righteousness is what gives us confidence on the day of judgment because we are cleansed and forgiven.

PERSONAL TAKE: Why can't fear and love coexist (v. 18)?

Fear has to do with punishment

PERSONAL REFLECTION: What do you most fear in your relationship with God? For instance, that He doesn't love you? That He can't forgive you? That you're not saved? That He's going to punish you? That judgment day will be condemning for you? List whatever comes to mind.

We fear we haven't done enough, which we haven't. We fear we're not good enough, which we're not. We fear we've sinned recklessly, which we have. We fear we don't have enough faith, which we don't. But verse 19 surpasses our countless fears and failures with a truth that trumps them all: We love because He first loved us.

PERSONAL RESPONSE: Looking back at the fears you listed, write how the truth of God's pursuing love for you silences each of those fears. Be specific.

"There is no fear in love; instead perfect love drives out fear, because fear involves punishment. So the one who fears has not reached perfection in love." (1 John 4:18, HCSB)

Let's look at this issue of fear another way. In the margin, name three things you would consider to be antonyms of fear:

1.

2.

3.

To the degree we're bound in fear we fail to grasp the love of God for us. I don't think I realized until recently how much my fear had kept me from the assurance I longed for, the peace, the comfort, the rest. I also don't think I realized how deeply my understanding of God's love for me is connected to my ability to love others.

John moves back into now familiar territory in verses 20-21. Select the two basic truths of this passage:

❏ If you love others you'll be healthier.

☑ If you love God you'll love others.

☑ You can't truly love God and hate your brother.

❏ You can't truly love God and hate chocolate.

Our love for God and our understanding of it directly affects our love for one another. We can't say we love God and hate our brother. Verse 21 cites the inverse: "anyone who loves God must also love their brother and sister." Here John gives us really obvious markers for our love for God, or lack of it. If we're bitter toward someone, unforgiving, angry, constantly in a bad mood, biting people's heads off, gossiping about others, irritated at them, we need to look at what is broken in our relationship with God, because loving God and loving others are inextricably connected. God's love for us goes before our love for others—loving others doesn't help us earn God's love, rather God's love for us grants us the capacity to love others. We love because He first loved us.

> Loving others doesn't help us earn God's love, rather God's love for us grants us the capacity to love others.

First John 4:20-21 is more closely connected to verses 17-19 than we may realize. God's love for us changes everything about the way we love others. So if you find yourself struggling to love, if you just can't find any more reserve, here's how I want to end today. Instead of dwelling on the person you're trying to love, dwell on the God who loved you first, and who in turn gives you the love to love that person.

PERSONAL RESPONSE: In your journal or on a separate sheet of paper, write a prayer of thanksgiving for the specific ways God's love has pursued you. This can include forgiveness of certain sins, the healing of a broken relationship, the hope you now have. Whatever comes to mind, just focus on His love for you.

DAY 5

TO LOVE IS TO OBEY

After spending several months in the epistles of 1, 2, and 3 John, I'm realizing that love is far more than I could have ever imagined it to be, but it is also far less. What I mean by more is that loving like Jesus loved means I'll sacrifice my personal comforts for another, I'll take on a friend's burden, forgive someone who betrayed me, feed a stranger, hold an orphan with a contagious bug, give my money away, pursue the person on the fringes of society—the one whose worldview and behavior are entirely different from mine.

By love being less I mean that true love doesn't require you to embrace every worldview, desire, or behavior that enters your sphere. This is not to suggest that love doesn't wildly pursue the sinner, but God's love is not a blank check that says "I'm OK, you're OK, so let's just support whatever whim or fancy anyone has under the umbrella of love." "Love has definite character and structure."[13]

If you tend toward judgment and pointing the finger, John is saying love is so much more than that! You need to get out there and love the people you're judging. If you tend toward the to-each-his-own mindset under the broad banner of love, John is saying, love is much narrower because it actually means something specific. In today's study we'll see how love is inextricably connected to obedience. To love God is to obey Him. As we open the last chapter of 1 John, my prayer is that today will fill you with hope and freedom you may not have known. We're one step of obedience away.

Read 1 John 5:1-5.

Ask the Holy Spirit to open your eyes so you can behold wondrous things from His Word (See Ps. 119:18.)

PERSONAL TAKE: Though John often circles back around to ideas previously mentioned, what is one new thought or idea you gained from these verses?

If I haven't mentioned it yet, or one hundred times, reading John sometimes makes me feel like I'm back in Algebra class trying to figure out those dreaded word problems. If this is true, and that is true, how many socks does Sally have in her top drawer that aren't rainbow colored, and will she have enough coins to buy a candy bar at the store?

So, we get another couplet in John's opening verse of chapter 5, hopefully simpler than a story problem.
"Everyone who believes that Jesus is the Christ (Messiah) is ___born of God___.
Everyone who loves the father loves ___his child as well___."

This second part wasn't totally clear to me until I studied it further, so here's what John is saying in a nutshell: If we say we love God we will also love His children (the church). Put another way, my friend who's adopting a child called me the other night to share the details of bringing her daughter home. I ended the phone call with, "I love you, so I will love her." Because I love my friend I will naturally love her child. John is carrying over his thoughts on loving God and loving others.

PERSONAL REFLECTION: Have you ever chosen to love another child of God simply because you loved God? You may not have had natural affection toward the person but because you loved God you loved the person. Jot down as much as you can about the situation without being offensive if anyone were to see your notes.

With what five words does verse 2 begin? They're quite familiar to us now: This is how we ___Know___.

This is the last time John will use this phrase, and it's a beautiful refrain. What two reasons does John give for how we can know that we love others, especially those who are in the body of Christ?

First Reason: ___by Loving God___

Second Reason: ___Carrying out his commands___

These merge together because in verse 3, John says that to love God is to carry out His commands. John's structure is a little complex at times, but his message here is straightforward: You can't divorce obeying God from loving Him. If we love Him we will obey Him.

I could cry over this passage, because obedience to Christ has been my greatest demonstration of my love for Him. Period. For me, obedience has at times meant intense loneliness. It's meant walking in the exact opposite direction of my hopes. It's meant doing what I didn't want to do and not doing what I wanted to. Obedience has required surrender. It's meant following Him above all my individual desires and dreams, so I can live the life for which He's created me. Today, I couldn't be more thankful to have chosen His way over my own, because it was at the table of obedience where I got to know Him. Obedience is where relationship with Christ is forged.

PERSONAL REFLECTION: What milestone marker of obedience especially proved your love for Jesus?

Not only does our obedience to God demonstrate our love for Him, it also shows our love for others. Look back at verse 2: "This is how we know that we love the Children of God."

PERSONAL TAKE: Name three specific ways that obeying God affects your love for His children.

1.

2.

3.

When I read this passage I immediately think of romantic relationships. I think of how often we say that we love the person we're with, meanwhile disregarding the commands God's given us to honor one another's bodies through sexual purity. How can a person say that she loves her boyfriend when she continually sins against him and herself by crossing the boundaries God has given? To truly love and honor the person we say we love is synonymous with obeying God's commands regarding sexual wholeness and purity. If we're married, obeying His commands means staying faithful to our spouse. If we're in a dating relationship, it means not giving ourselves away sexually—equally, not receiving another's body sexually—until marriage. In our culture this may seem like torture at worst and just plain antiquated at least, but here's where John sweeps in with the most refreshing breeze of good news.

According to verse 3, what are God's commands NOT? (I had to capitalize this word, because this is the best ever.)

Burdensome –

For a fuller understanding, the Greek word here is *barys*, and it means *heavy in weight, burdensome, severe, cruel, unsparing.*

> **PERSONAL TAKE:** Think of a person carrying a 50-pound load over her shoulder. In what different ways would that load affect her as she went through her day? (Don't skip this question because I know you want to. Give it some thought.)

Let's now look at another place in the New Testament where this exact word is used, followed by a passage that sheds light on the idea.

- Read Matthew 23:1-4. What did the Pharisees (religious leaders) of the day put on the shoulders of their followers?

  heavy Loads –

- Read Acts 15:10-11. What does Peter suggest is the exact opposite of trying to live under a heavy yoke of excessive law-keeping to earn salvation?

  Through grace of Christ we are Saved.

> **PERSONAL TAKE:** After seeing two references of what burdensome or grievous loads of legalism can look like, what do you think sets God's commands apart?

The thought of God's commands as not burdensome is interesting because who hasn't felt at one time or another that obeying one of God's commands might literally kill you? Even so, something being hard, difficult, or even painful doesn't necessarily mean burdensome.

God's commands will never weigh us down; rather, they set us free. His commands won't slow our pace or sap our strength with guilt, consequences, and remorse. To love God is to obey Him, and to obey Him means running unfettered through the open fields of His blessing, even if we have to deny our flesh to get there. Psalm 119:32 says, "I run in the path of your commands, for you have set my heart free" (1984 NIV).

PERSONAL REFLECTION: Briefly describe a scenario where an act of obedience was hard for you but the blessing of walking in His commandments proved *light,* as in *not burdensome.*

I just finished up a health cleanse that lasted for 30 days. The author of the plan states at the beginning of the book, "Please don't tell us this program is hard." She lovingly continues, "[tragedies are] hard. Drinking your coffee black. Is. Not. Hard."[14] I had to smile because I'd already thought about how precisely hard it was going to be to not have milk in my coffee for 30 days. But the author was saying, this is for your good, you big baby. You're getting to take charge of your health. You can do this! Don't tell me this is hard.

I totally got her point, but am so thankful that John adds something more for those of us who absolutely do not have what it takes to obey in our own strength. The obedience God demands is not just about us pulling ourselves up by our own bootstraps, digging deep, getting our obedience game on. In 1 John 5:4-5, John goes on to add an important component to our obedience.

What does John say is our victory in overcoming the world?
- ☑ faith
- ❑ will power
- ❑ inner strength
- ❑ joy

PERSONAL TAKE: John defines faith as those who believe in Jesus as the Son of God. Through that faith we are spiritually reborn. Comparing John 16:33 with 1 John 5:4, what does spiritual rebirth have to do with overcoming the world?

you may have peace — Christ has overcome

Our ability to overcome the pulls and temptations of the world begins with Christ and the reality that He's already overcome. This is not the easiest concept to explain, but I can emphatically tell you it can be experienced. All of us will be faced with situations where obeying will seem beyond our ability. It's here where we submit our hearts to God's loving rule and way and then experience the power that comes from being born of God. We'll look back and see strongholds demolished, strength for our weakness, and beauty for the ashes. And we'll ever so slightly glimpse the mystery of what happens when our frail choice to obey links arms with His power to overcome. And we'll know the victory that is our faith in Jesus.

This may prove one of the most important days in our study of 1, 2, and 3 John. It's vital because if we're in a state of active disobedience in any area it will affect our love for God, spilling over into our love for others.

> **PERSONAL RESPONSE:** Pondering the immense love God has for us woven through chapters 4 and 5, confess any area of disobedience to the Lord. If it's a place of repeated failure, meditate on the truth of being an overcomer in Jesus.

Instead of dwelling on how hard obedience to Jesus feels in the moment, dwell on how much your obedience proves that you love Him. I love what the late Dallas Willard says about this: "One of the lies about the spiritual life is that it is hard. No, no. It is not hard. It is the easy way. What's hard is the other way, and that is what you see when you look at the world."[15]

I couldn't be any happier for the progress you've made. The concepts we've explored this week have not been easy and you've done an amazing job remaining with the study. I've decided that figuring out what John means can be a real challenge, but what's even more challenging is when you do understand him: loving others like Christ loves us, laying down our lives for our brothers and sisters, walking in the light, testing the spirits, driving out fear with love.

None of this is easy stuff, and yet when we're walking with Jesus, nothing on earth will prove easier than His yoke or lighter than His burden (see Matt. 11:28-30). Because His commands are not burdensome.

KALE, SAUSAGE, AND CANNELLINI BEAN SOUP
FROM THE KITCHEN OF KELLY MINTER

My friends and family give me a hard time for my addiction to soup-making. I can't help it—fresh ingredients, simmering pots, the cathartic motion of stirring. Plus, the health benefits are stellar, especially if you can make your own broth (but I'm getting ahead of myself). I love this soup because it's both nutritious and satisfying. The sausage adds a hearty flavor, the beans give texture, and the kale offers health benefits (and vegetable popularity for the moment). You'll love this soup.

INGREDIENTS
- 1/4 cup extra-virgin olive oil
- 6 to 8 cloves garlic, thinly sliced
- 2 teaspoons dried oregano
- 1 (6-ounce) can tomato paste
- 2 tablespoons red wine vinegar
- Shaved parmesan cheese for on top
- 2 (15-ounce) cans cannellini beans, drained and rinsed
- 2 1/2 quarts chicken stock (more if you want a brothier soup)
- 1 lb of Italian sausage (I prefer 4 sausage links)
- 1 large bunch kale, large ribs removed, chopped
- Salt and freshly ground black pepper

DIRECTIONS
1. Heat oil in a large pot.
2. Add garlic and oregano and sauté until translucent.
3. Add vinegar and tomato paste, and cook another minute until the oil and paste has blended together.
4. Add rinsed beans and stock and bring to a simmer. (At this point I let the soup simmer for about 30-45 minutes before adding the kale because I don't like my kale overcooked—this is just a preference.)
5. Season with salt and pepper, to taste.
6. While the soup is simmering, in another pan I partially cook the sausage links (you can also use ground sausage). Once halfway cooked, I allow them to cool and then I slice them into bite-sized pieces and toss them into the soup where they finish cooking. I like for the sausage to cook a bit in the soup because you get a fuller flavor in the broth.
7. Add kale and simmer, partially covered, for another 15-30 minutes or so, making sure of course the sausage is thoroughly cooked.
8. Garnish with fresh shaved Parmesan cheese.

CREAMY CHICKEN AVOCADO ENCHILADAS

FROM THE KITCHEN OF CARRIE E.

INGREDIENTS

- 2 Tbsp. olive oil
- 1 medium white or yellow onion, diced fine
- 1 can of green chilis
- 8-10 corn or flour tortillas
- 4 cups shredded cooked chicken
- 2-3 cups Monterrey Jack cheese
- fresh cilantro to top it off
- Avocado Cream Sauce Ingredients:
- 2 Tbsp. butter
- 2 Tbsp. rice flour or regular flour
- 2 cups chicken broth
- ¾ cup sour cream
- ½ tsp. cumin
- ½ tsp. garlic powder
- ½ tsp. salt
- ¼ tsp. pepper
- 2 Avocados
- ½ cup chopped fresh cilantro
- juice of one lime

INSTRUCTIONS

1. First make the avocado cream sauce:
2. Melt the butter in a skillet over medium high heat. Add the flour and whisk it continuously until golden and bubbly, about 2-3 minutes.
3. Slowly whisk the broth into the flour mixture. Bring to a boil, then reduce heat to medium-low and simmer for 5 minutes.
4. Add the sour cream, cumin, salt, garlic powder and pepper, whisking to remove lumps.
5. Remove from heat and let cool for a few minutes. Transfer mixture to a blender or food processor. Add avocados, cilantro and lime juice, and pulse until smooth and well-blended.
6. Season with additional salt or pepper if needed.
7. In a large skillet, heat olive oil over medium-high heat. Add onion, and saute for 5-6 minutes until the onions are cooked and translucent.
8. Stir in your green chilis.
9. Remove from heat.
10. Spread a couple tablespoons of the avocado sauce down the middle of a tortilla. Then layer on some of the vegetable mixture, shredded chicken and cheese.
11. Roll the tortilla and place it seam side down in the baking dish and repeat with the rest of your tortillas.
12. Drizzle the top with about half of the remaining avocado cream sauce, then cover the dish with foil and bake for about 20 minutes in a 350 degree oven, or until tortillas are heated through and begin to harden.

Remove from oven and drizzle the remaining avocado sauce and garnish with cilantro and enjoy!

EXPERIENCING THE WORD

I'd been in the Amazon jungles of Brazil for over a week. The culture was almost feeling familiar to me—all these laid-back people floating through life, winding and meandering as languidly as the Amazon River itself. Trying to keep Brazilians on a schedule is like trying to keep a Golden Retriever from licking you. It's wonderful and maddening. Their general way of life forces me to slow down and embrace the present moment, which is why I've come to believe that being around Brazilians for days at a time is not only for my pure enjoyment, but also for my personal sanctification. They are a sensory, celebratory bunch ready to slap on a party hat at a moment's notice.

My Brazilian friend Francie whisked my other friend Mary Katharine and me into a grocery store in Manaus. Liters of Coca-Cola® bottles in specialized colors lined the checkout conveyor belt, strategically placed for impulse buyers. I asked Francie what the Portuguese slogan on the labels said.

"Oh, Kelly," she said, "they say 'Together, Let's Color Brazil.'" Mary Katharine and I just stared at her. "You know?" she motioned with her hands, "Together we can color Brazil!" As if saying it again would somehow help us get it. To her credit she kept trying…. "Like, Kelly," she explained, "We can paint the city!" Her expression grew brighter. "We can come together and bring color!"

I watched the bags of rice and powdered milk we were buying for a friend in the jungle roll down the conveyor belt. I still had no idea what she was talking about; in that moment I was too American for my own good. All I could think was that if this grocery store were in Nashville the Coke® bottles would have said something like, "Together, we can educate America," or "Together, we can build a better future." I'm not exactly sure, but it wouldn't be "let's color the place."

The next morning Francie told me she couldn't sleep the night before trying to figure out another way to get the sentiment across. She wanted me to understand her culture, to embrace the message of the Coke® bottles. Though I couldn't have defined what coloring Brazil—all together now—technically meant in scientific or formulaic terms, after so many trips to Manaus, a part of me did understand. And it's the very thing I love about Brazilians. They're passionate and sensory. Give them an experience or give them death. As Francie and I went back and forth about our differing cultures, the whole thing escalated to the two of us hung over in laughter that something as vague and esoteric as a slogan could inspire such effort to discuss and grasp.

Sometimes when reading John's letters I feel like I'm back in that Brazilian grocery store staring blankly at Portuguese, my head slightly cocked. Even when I'm given explanations in commentaries, concordances, and dictionaries, I'm still often left squinting, staring, yanking at my hair. Part of this is because John's message and style are unique. His letters are quite different from Paul's, whose epistles I primarily grew up on during Sunday sermons. And John's Gospel is markedly different from Matthew, Mark, and Luke's (also known as the Synoptic Gospels). And who can claim to have a rock solid handle on Revelation? So I'm finding myself in somewhat new territory as I spend this much time in John's world—fresh ground that is both challenging and thrilling. I'm starting to get a feel for how he thinks and what's important to him. I'm enjoying studying the words and phrases uniquely his, and I hope you are too.

We've acquainted ourselves with words like *propitiation*. We've studied what John means when he tells us to not love the world, and who exactly he's referring to when he calls his readers children, young men, and fathers. We've been introduced to the old command and in the next breath John called it a new command, almost as if he changed his mind midstream. He's seamlessly bounced from light and dark, love and hate, and sometimes we have trouble following his train of thought. But then in a burst of insight we'll have an encounter in a quiet moment with the Lord, or fellowshipping around the dinner table, or we'll read an article or hear a story, and we'll think, *Maybe that's what John meant when he said …*

This week we'll continue to pull some Greek words apart, and we'll compare other parts of Scripture in hopes of shedding light on John's letters. We'll work our way through the verses slowly and we'll do our best to apprehend John's meanings. We'll read quotes from scholars and occasionally dig our thumbs into our eyebrows because we're still not quite sure what this or that means.

All of this is good because we'll be doing our best to rightly divide the Word of Truth, as the author of Timothy puts it. But in our diligence and zeal to understand, there will be no substitute for time spent. If you have the time, allow yourself the freedom to rabbit trail into John's Gospel, comparing and contrasting the accounts of Jesus with John's letters. Ask the Lord to give you understanding that goes beyond technical study. Certainly the words of John can be properly explained, studied, even distilled. But we can never forget that his words were written primarily to be experienced. And this is worth coloring the country. All together.

VIEWER GUIDE

ABIDE, DWELL, REMAIN

Jesus is the _____Vine_____

God, the Father is the _____gardener_____

GROUP DISCUSSION QUESTIONS:

How does your daily reality reflect the premise that the pressure is off you and on Jesus as the vine and His Father as the gardener? In what ways do you see yourself constantly striving, fretting, and attempting to control?

How have you experienced the truth that obeying God doesn't earn God's love but obedience does allow us to walk more fully in the benefits of His love? (See John 15:9.)

John wrote that we are overcomers because of Jesus. If you feel comfortable, encourage the group by share about something the Lord helped you overcome, something you couldn't have overcome on your own. (p. 107-108)

Describe a situation where you distinctly felt different from the world and its desires— where you realized how not-of-this-world you really are (p. 109).

What do you most fear in your relationship with God? (p. 116) How does the fact that the love of God casts out fear bring assurance in your relationship with God? (p. 114-115)

WATER, BLOOD, AND SPIRIT

It was a lonely season for me. A bleak one, really. The astounding beauty of Estes Park, Colorado where I was singing for the weekend did little to lift the sadness and worry inside me. I strolled through the quaint town and ordered lunch at a restaurant. While waiting for my meal an odd sort of woman sat down next to me—I am the strongest magnet for odd you've ever seen. Somehow we started talking about Jesus and she mentioned today's passage. How Jesus had come through water and blood and how the Spirit testifies to this. I remember I hardly understood a word she said and to this day I don't know if she was an angel sent to encourage me or just a really different sort of woman. I lean toward the latter. Either way, all these years later here we are studying this passage and it's a fascinating one, if not a little dense. But we're used to dense at this point. Read 1 John 5:6-13.

By what two ways did Jesus come? _Water_ and _Blood_

This reference would have been easily understood by the readers of John's day, but for us this is not nearly as clear. With some historical background and a bit of cross-referencing I'm hopeful we can make good sense of what John's referring to here. More than anything, I hope our lives will be impacted by it. Let's take both of these individually:

Water

According to Matthew 3:1-2,4-6,11, what act of the heart accompanied those who were being baptized?

Confessing their Sins

Who descended upon Jesus after His baptism (see Matt. 3:13-17)?

Spirit of God.

Since Jesus was sinless, what reason did He give for being baptized?

fulfull all righteousness

When John says that Jesus came by *water,* he's most likely referring to Jesus' baptism. He humbly identified with us when He participated in water baptism, even though He was without sin. As well, this marked the official beginning of Jesus' ministry, a historical act that John is pointing His readers to in our text today.

Some scholars believe the water and blood signify baptism and the Lord's Supper. Others believe they represent the water and blood that flowed from Christ's side when He was pierced on the cross.

Blood

Notice the emphasis John puts on the blood when he says Jesus didn't only come by water but by water and blood. As you read the following verses keep in mind that under the old covenant animals were sacrificed and their blood was used to atone for the sin of the one making the sacrifice. Read Hebrews 9:11-14.

By whose blood did Jesus enter The Most Holy Place on our behalf?

by his own Blood —

What does the shedding of blood accomplish (see Heb. 9:22)?

forgiveness

The idea of animal blood sacrifices is hard to bear in our culture. We hardly recognize a chicken breast with the skin on and bone in, much less anything with blood on it. The sacrifice of a person's blood is even harder for us to fathom. But refresh your memory with 1 John 1:7.

What comes as a result of the glorious blood of Jesus?

Purifies us from all Sin —

PERSONAL RESPONSE: After reading about the water and blood, finish the statements in the margin. Don't worry about right answers, just your answers.

John's mention of water and blood here may very well have been to refute some of the false beliefs of the day. We've talked about some of the pre-gnostic views, those who didn't believe Jesus was fully human as well as those who didn't believe He was fully divine. Interestingly, a prominent figure of John's day named Cerinthus believed that the heavenly Christ descended on Jesus at His baptism but later withdrew from Him before the cross. This denied Jesus' divinity, instead believing He was simply a human figure upon whom the Christ came temporarily. "All the force of … 'God showed his love to us' by sending his Son to die disappears if the One who died was not in fact Jesus Christ.'"[1]

Jesus didn't only identify with us through water baptism, He also came by blood, which cost Him His life. "If the Son of God did not take to himself our nature in his birth and our sins in his death, he cannot reconcile us to God. So John emphasizes not just that he came, but especially that he came by water and blood, since it is his blood which cleanses us from sin."[2]

I just realized we're not even all the way through verse 6. I don't even know what to say about this except that John can't be rushed. Reading

Jesus coming by water reminds me that …

Confessing sins.

Jesus coming by blood is meaningful to me because …

forgiveness.

him is slower than trying to get out of the house with your glasses and keys. John won't get out the door if he can squeeze two more enormous theologies into two more words, like *water* and *blood*. See? I cannot be blamed for this pace. Re-read verses 6-9.

What defining word does verse 6 say that the Holy Spirit is?
❑ charity   ❑ faith   ☑ truth   ❑ grace

What significant role does the Holy Spirit play in this passage?
Testifies -

PERSONAL REFLECTION: Have you ever had to testify (or bear witness) to something in a serious matter? If so, what influence did your testimony have? Respond in the margin.

In summation, John is saying that not only do two physical acts point to Jesus as Savior, His baptism (*water*) and the cross (*blood*), but also the Holy Spirit testifies to this truth. Consider how important His testimony is. Have you ever doubted if Jesus really came? Have you ever felt so undone by your sin and past that you wondered if Jesus' blood could truly purify you? Have you experienced a tragedy that suddenly made you wonder if everything you believed about Jesus was even real? What about a college course that almost upended your faith? John gives us assurance through a real, living person: the Holy Spirit. This may seem nebulous because we're not used to listening for His voice or recognizing His affirmations. But since reading this passage I've been asking the Holy Spirit to help me discern His testimony, the one He's still proclaiming.

Turn to chapter 14 of John's Gospel and picture the setting. Jesus is speaking to His disciples right before His death. John is a young man at the time who's been following Jesus as one of His disciples. Jesus explains that He's going to leave them for the Father, much to the disciples' sadness and shock. Comforting them, Jesus reminds them of a Counselor, the Holy Spirit, that the Father will send in His absence. As you read Jesus' words, remember John was there. He was one of the few to whom these words were directly spoken.

Read John 14:25-26. What did Jesus say the Holy Spirit would remind them of? *everyThing Jesus had said*

Jesus said that the Holy Spirit would "live ___*with*___ you and be ___*in*___ you" (John 14:15-17).

Jesus says the Holy Spirit will take from what is Jesus' and ___*Make it Known to you*___ (John 16:7,13-15).

Jesus came by water and blood (1 John 5:6)

WHAT LOVE IS

Before Jesus went to the Father He comforted His disciples with the incredible gift of the Holy Spirit, even going so far as to say it was good that He go away so He could send the Spirit.

PERSONAL REFLECTION: What characteristic or role of the Holy Spirit means the most to you at this time in your life, and why?

Go back to 1 John. Re-read verses 5:9-10. Yesterday I went to the airport to witness my friend bring her new adopted daughter home. I along with about 50 others can testify that she walked past security with her child bound up in her arms. I held her, I swept my thumb across her cheek, we sang "Deep and Wide" together, I watched her eat her first cookie on American soil.

When Missy grows up I'll tell her about this day, because I was there. I witnessed it. If you accept my testimony about this day, how much more is John saying that we should accept the very testimony of God?

Who is God's testimony about? (v. 9)

Testimony of God

When I consider that God, through the Holy Spirit, is actually giving testimony about who Jesus is, I'm amazed. Dear reader, He's still speaking. He's still telling us all about Him. Ask Him for ears to hear His testimony (see Mark 4:23).

PERSONAL RESPONSE: What about Jesus do you doubt? Write your prayer asking the Holy Spirit to reveal His testimony of Jesus to you. Remember, as a believer, this testimony is already in your heart (see v. 10).

Re-read verses 11-12, where John sums this up beautifully. Fill in the rest of the phrase. "This is the testimony God has given about His Son…

He who has the Son has Life
He who does not have the Son of God does not have Life

When you think of the myriad world religions, the latest fad beliefs, the countless claims about God, John boils God's testimony down to a single phrase: God has given us eternal life in Jesus. The accessibility, the simplicity, the unbelievable goodness of it all. Salvation is found in no other name (see Acts 4:12). Jesus is the only way to God (see John 14:6).

- John closes this passage with one of his now famous couplets:
- Whoever has the _Son_ has _Life_
- Whoever does not have the _Son_ does not have _Life_

What is more important than life itself? Jesus even asked the question, "what good is it for you to gain the world but lose your soul?" (see Mark 8:34). The life Jesus is talking about surely includes our physical life in the here and now, but He is speaking of the fuller life of relationship with God, purified from our sins and in communion with Him. Life that won't end when we draw our last breath. Life that is eternal. This is the very testimony of God about Jesus! In perfect Johannine form John says you either have Him or you don't. And the best news ever is that today, you can have Him.

PERSONAL RESPONSE: OPTION 1 If you know you have life in Jesus, will you take a sacred moment to consider the life He's freed you to live? Don't rush this time.

PERSONAL RESPONSE: OPTION 2 If you've never known true life, or been confused about what you needed to do or believe, here it is. As simple as it can be. Believe in the Son of God, the One who is the atoning sacrifice for your sins (1 John 4:10), who loved you first. If you have come to believe Him today, write out a prayer of belief below.

If today you wrote out a prayer of belief, in the words of John himself, you have "passed from death unto life" (1 John 3:14). Welcome, dear child. Welcome.

What better way to begin our week together than being reminded that John has written these things to us so that we can know that we have eternal life (v. 13). Embrace the idea that when it comes to something as essential as eternal life, we don't have to guess, wonder, strive, hope, or grasp. We can know.

Eternal life is a reality we can know we possess (1 John 5:13)

ASKING ACCORDING TO HIS WILL

When I was four years old I started asking my mom questions about Jesus. I'd heard in Sunday school about His forgiveness and love for me. At one point she asked me if I was ready to receive Him as my personal Savior. "Not yet," I said.

"Why not?"

"Because I don't understand the whole Bible yet." So. That was the end of that conversation for a while.

Fortunately we don't have to understand the whole Bible to come to know Jesus, just as we don't have to understand everything about prayer to pray. But as we enter today's passage on prayer I'll admit that I wish I understood it more. I wanted to have this one locked down before writing about it. But I'll tell you something you probably already knew: I don't have prayer totally down yet. Thankfully the Word is so powerful, far beyond my ability to understand or teach it, so I don't have to fully grasp the text for us to be ministered to by it.

Read 1 John 5:14-15. Begin with verse 5:13 if you like. Some translations treat verse 13 as a closing thought to the previous section (which I did), while others use it to open the following section. Either way, knowing we have eternal life is a wonderful reminder as we consider prayer.

Some of you have been praying for something that has yet to be answered, like for children, a spouse, a health condition to improve, a better job. Or you may have prayed for things that were simply not answered the way you'd pleaded, perhaps for the healing of a loved one. Based on your experiences, are you fearful to continue hoping in prayer based on an "unanswered" prayer? Do you doubt your amount of faith? Do you think if you'd been more disciplined in prayer God may have responded more favorably?

PERSONAL REFLECTION: In the margin write any thoughts you have. These will be important as we continue today's study.

Let's begin with verse 14. When we approach God in prayer, what is our confidence based on?

- ❑ our faith
- ❑ our goodness
- ☑ that He hears us
- ❑ how early we rise to pray

When it comes to prayer it's easy for our needs and wants to take precedence and become the centerpiece. But John says, wait, let's pause a moment here. Consider that the God of the universe hears you. Before we get to a plea or petition—even a praise—let's just revel in the reality that God hears us in the first place. I like what one author says, "'If we know that He hears us, whatever we request,' it is enough."[3]

> **PERSONAL RESPONSE:** Do you ever doubt that God hears your prayers? If so, how does this negatively affect what you pray for and how often you pray?

Can you see how the Enemy can use a simple lie like, God doesn't actually hear you when you pray, to discourage an effective prayer life?

> Psalm 135:15-17 speaks to how personal the God of the Bible is versus idols made by human hands. Read these verses and in the margin list four features idols have and four things they cannot do.

1. *Mouth / Speak*
2. *eyes – See*
3. *ears – hear*
4. *breath · breath*

The following passages all have to do with God hearing us. Look up each one and answer the corresponding question.

> **2 CHRONICLES 7:14** Is there anything you need to confess to God? If so, write it below or on separate paper.

> **PSALM 34:17** Who does the Lord hear in this instance?
> *righteous*
> **PSALM 55:17 TRUE/FALSE:** The best time to cry out to the Lord is when you've got everything together.
> *when in distress –*
> **PSALM 116:1-2** The Lord hears our cries for ___*Mercy*___.

I hope we've established that the confidence we have in prayer comes from the fact that He hears us. But this doesn't mean our beliefs or behavior are inconsequential. Let's take a brief Scriptural survey of effectual prayer.

TRUE/FALSE: According to 1 John 5:14, we can ask of God whatever we want according to our will and He'll do it. *No... his will*

Look back at 1 John 3:21-23. John mentions a couple additional insights into receiving from God whatever we ask. What are they?

If our heart does not Condemn us.
He Knows every thing!

Now turn to John's Gospel, verses 15:7-8. When it comes to answered prayer, Jesus describes a state of being that includes two realities:

• We must remain in ____*him*____
• His ____*Words*____ must remain in us.

PERSONAL TAKE: What do these two mutual realities mean as they relate to prayer? Give this some thought.

Now turn over to James 4:2-3. What does James say is wrong with the way we sometimes pray?

We don't Ask God ...

Here's a list of what we've gathered so far:

- Our confidence in prayer is based on the reality that God hears us.

- We have what we ask of Him when we ask according to His will.

- When our lifestyle is characterized by obedience and doing the things that please God, we receive from Him anything we ask.

- What we ask will be given to us when Jesus' words remain in us and we remain in Him.

- When our only desire in prayer is to fulfill our passions and pleasures, we won't receive what we ask for. *Wrong motives*

PERSONAL REFLECTION: What one specific truth from these passages challenges or encourages you to pray more fervently?

When we pray according to God's will He hears us and we know that we have what we asked of Him (1 John 5:14-15)

So we're getting a clearer picture of what it means to receive anything we ask for in Jesus' name. Asking in Jesus' name doesn't mean a carte blanche request for whatever we want. But I believe it means far more than what most of us claim it to mean. We tend to focus on what it's not because many of us have been disappointed by prayer, or we feel the need to draw a line between ourselves and the name-it-claim-ers. But instead of looking at everything this passage doesn't mean, I wonder what would happen if we considered all it does mean? Andrew Murray wrote, "Beware in your prayers, above everything else, of limiting God, not only by unbelief, but by fancying that you know what He can do."[4]

PERSONAL RESPONSE: Have you made 1 John 5:14-15 less than it says? If so, at what point do you not believe what John is saying?

I recently celebrated the 79th birthday of a dear friend's mother, Donna. She has taken prayer walks in many parts of the world. She is a prayer warrior of warriors. She prays for the nations, the state she lives in, the capitol of the state, the justices that preside over the capitol, all the way down to her children, grandchildren, and great-grandchildren. So over dinner I took the opportunity to talk to her about 1 John 5:14-15— because I know this is what she wanted to talk about on her birthday.

"What does it mean," I asked her "when John says whatever we ask of Him, we know that we have what we asked?" She said: "I take those verses very literally. We are His beloved, and He longs to give us what we ask for. He delights in it! And He wants so much more for us than we can even imagine." So of course I asked her what happens when we ask for things that we absolutely believe are according to God's will that don't turn out as we prayed. She experienced the loss of her only son so she's well acquainted with life not going the way you hope and pray. "Our minds are so finite," she reminded me. "We're so limited in our understanding that often when God answers prayer His answer looks different than what we had in mind. But this doesn't mean He's not answering in the best possible way." Donna's husband Jack also chimed in. "And we as humans are on a certain timetable, but God's timetable is entirely different than ours. So prayer also requires patience."

PERSONAL REFLECTION: Describe a time when you prayed for something and God answered your prayer in an entirely different way than you could have imagined, yet you are now thankful for it.

As I close this day of study, know I'll be pondering these two verses in 1 John for a long time. While I'm not entirely sure of all these verses hold, I know they mean a whole lot more than I've believed them for. The bottom line is that I ask too little of the Lord and I ask too narrowly. Little, in that I don't ask for more, and narrow in that—as Andrew Murray says—I limit Him to what I think He can do. Ask in His name. Ask according to His will. Delight Him with your obedience. Have confidence that He hears you. And see what He will do.

DAY 3
PRAYERS THAT GIVE LIFE

Every Sunday my pastor greets our congregation by saying, "We study through books of the Bible at our church." Pastor Jim likes this approach because it forces him, as well as us, to deal with whatever verses come our way. This can be both wonderful and difficult; wonderful when you're in the Gospels talking about Jesus healing someone, difficult when you're in Judges and a man named Ehud thrusts his sword through a king named Eglon and the sword gets stuck in Eglon's fat. (We covered this on Sunday).

Today is one of those more difficult days in our study through 1 John, or perhaps *perplexing* might be the better word. I do believe there are some encouraging treasures for us, though, and once we look at the verses in the context of the broader counsel of God's Word I'm hopeful we'll come away encouraged. Read 1 John 5:16-17.

First I want to set you at ease if you may be troubled by these verses, if you are a little like me. If you're wondering if you've already committed the sin that leads to death, I want you to see a couple verses for yourself.

How does God respond to those who call on His name? (See Rom. 10:13.)

they will be saved —

What is Jesus' promise for the person who believes in His words and trusts in God who sent Him? (See John 5:24.)

eternal Life

We'll address the difficulties of this passage, but I didn't want you fretting the whole time about whether you've committed the one, big sin that leads to death or that your season of habitual sin lasted one day longer than the maximum allowed by God's mercy. Just take a deep breath. Now, back to 1 John where we'll begin with verse 16.

> Who is John talking about in this verse?
> "If anyone sees his ___*brother*___ commit a sin …"
>
> What does John say we should do for that person? *Pray*
>
> What is the result of that action?
>   *God will give him life*

Some scholars believe *brother* means *fellow believer*. Others think the term is general, including nominal believers or even unbelievers. But let's lay that aside for now. First of all, John is not talking about appointing ourselves as the moral police, spying on people's actions. He's talking about a verifiable situation of blatant sin. Second, he tells us to pray, "not point fingers, turn a blind eye, initiate gossip, or bask in a feeling of superiority."[5] How many times have we engaged in one of these four instead of praying? I'm not even going to comment here. Third, the result of our prayer is that God will give this person life. This is incredible news!

The problem is, this amazing sequence of truths suddenly becomes a blur the minute we see the sin-that-leads-to-death part. We just freak out and forget everything John has just said because what could be worse than having committed the sin that leads to death? But let's just stay where we're at for the moment and we'll get to that part in a minute.

> Mark the approximate percentage of your prayer life that's devoted to interceding for someone who's caught in sin. This is not for the purpose of condemnation, at all. This is just an assessment.
>
> |---|---|---|---|---|---|---|---|---|---|---|
> 0%   10%   20%   30%   40%   50%   60%   70%   80%   90%   100%
>
> When you know someone who's actively involved in a sin, how effective do you believe your prayers are in changing the situation?
> ❑ The person I know is too far gone for prayer.
> ❑ I know prayer can change things, but honestly I don't have much hope in this situation.
> ❑ I believe prayer makes a difference but I'm not motivated enough to really go after it.
> ❑ I absolutely believe God can use my prayers to deliver someone.

A new friend shared about her sister who recently came to faith in Christ. My friend explained that one of the only prayers she'd consistently prayed over her life was that her sister would come to know the Lord. This seemed improbable since her sister used to burn Bibles, had become a drug addict and wanted nothing to do with church or Christians. Recently hitting rock bottom she went to a church service where the pastor felt God calling him to set his sermon aside and instead pray for all those who were dealing with drug and sexual addiction and who'd gone through the pain of an abortion. My friend's sister wept uncontrollably the entire service. My friend's seemingly unlikely prayer had been answered: Her sister gave her life to Jesus.

> **PERSONAL RESPONSE:** Because prayer is best understood when practiced, take a few minutes to privately pray for someone you know who's walking in darkness. I can think of a few people whom—I'll confess—I've given up praying for. These words from John have renewed my belief that prayer can absolutely affect them. But here's the thing, I have to actually do it.

I definitely think it's worth turning to James 5:13-20. Read these verses and consider them as if they might actually be true. James ends his letter by telling us to remember something very important.

> How does what James tells us compare to 1 John 5:16?
>
> James 5:20 "Whoever turns a sinner from the error of his way will save him from ___death___."
>
> 1 John 5:16 "If anyone sees a brother commit a sin…he should pray and God will give him ___life___."

When we pray a sinner to repentance it's a double blessing. The person is delivered from darkness, and they're delivered into light. I'm so grateful for the challenge and hope here. We are not powerless bystanders while our friends and loved ones get tangled up in affairs, pornography, alcoholism, food addiction, sexual immorality, false religions, petty gossip, or materialism. We're invited into the mysterious work of seeing people saved from death because God grants life. If we'll pray!

Let's get on our hands and knees for those we've given up hope for because we've believed too little about what God is capable of doing: trading sin and death for holiness and life. Let's get out our list of names that we've been lazy about praying over, people we've ceased trusting

God can change. Let's not have it be said of us that, "we have in fact become so unconcerned about the sins of our fellow Christians that we have ceased even to think about praying for them."[6]

> Personal Response: Either here or in a private journal, will you name three people who are actively living in sin? And will you commit to praying that God will give those people life?

Okay, now, let's look at the last part of verse 16:

> **PERSONAL TAKE:** Based on 1 John so far, what do you think John means when he says: "There is a sin that leads to death"? Think about the context of the antichrists, what John's written about sin, forgiveness, our Advocate, etc. Respond in the margin.

As already mentioned, I believe it's well supported that John is not talking about one specific heinous sin. Some believe he is talking about blasphemy of the Holy Spirit (see Matt. 12:31-32), or apostasy. My personal leaning is to take our cues from what John has already talked about in his letter. "It is plain that the author is most concerned about the sins which are incompatible with being a child of God, and these are summed up in denial that Jesus is the Son of God, refusal to obey God's commands, love of the world, and hatred of one's brothers."[7]

John clearly lays out that sin leading to spiritual death exists. And while we must not soften this reality, John's whole letter is based on a more powerful reality—Jesus, the atoning sacrifice for our sins (see 1 John 2:2). My personal belief is that the sin that leads to death can be any sin that ultimately leads a person down the path to rejection of Jesus Christ. That's why at the top of today's study I wanted to set at ease those who seek and love Jesus—not because I have any power to do so, but because based on all John has already written, those who are in Christ cannot possibly be living in sin that leads to death. I hope this is making the tiniest bit of sense.

> How does John instruct us to pray for those who are living in sin that leads to death? (Look at his comments closely.)

John is somewhat vague about how to pray in this situation. You get the sense that he's leaving the decision to the readers as a matter between them and God. John may not have wanted to weigh in too heavily on how a person should pray, because only God knows the heart.

A close friend continued to pray for an ex-boyfriend who'd clearly walked away from the Lord, been unfaithful to her, had no regard for Scripture, and generally wreaked havoc in her life. A wonderfully wise older woman finally encouraged my friend, "It's time to stop praying for him." Hear me clearly. She wasn't saying the ex-boyfriend was beyond God's mercy or redemption. But the Lord had delivered my friend from that toxic relationship and she needed to be free from the attachment of even interceding for him. It was time to let go. I can't say for certain that this is what John had in mind, but I have felt released by the Holy Spirit from praying for certain people at certain times.

I sure hope that I in no way sound as if I'm encouraging anyone to stop praying for another person. John's major directive here is to pray, pray, pray. Our sisters and brothers who are caught in sin need our prayers so God can grant life. The much lesser underscored thought is that there may be times when we need to direct our prayers elsewhere. Let the Holy Spirit lead you, and be wise in your prayers. If you take anything away from today, take the power of interceding for others with you! Don't give up hope for the list you came up with.

Lastly, I'll leave you with a few of my own thoughts. I hope they help.

1. Keep all of Scripture in mind when interpreting verse 16. The Gospels, Paul's Epistles, Acts, Hebrews—they all point to salvation by grace. They point to unmerited favor and forgiveness even for the most wicked. Even Paul said he was chief among sinners.

2. Also, keep in mind what you've already learned from John's letters. He acknowledges that we all sin and that Jesus Christ purifies and saves us from that sin because of His atonement for us. So keep the immediate context in mind.

3. Remember that John is encouraging prayer here. The main idea of these verses is that we pray for our brothers and sisters, not that we get in a knot over the sin that leads to death.

4. John's readers would have surely known exactly what sin John meant. Part of what makes this difficult is we're a couple thousand years removed from the time and circumstances of John's writing.

5. While there is a sin that leads to death there is a Savior who leads to life and anyone who calls on His name will be saved.

DAY 4

KNOWING A THING OR THREE

Today is one of those days where I would love for you to pore over the text a few minutes before I share any of my thoughts. If you were in any way thrown by yesterday's reading, you'll appreciate the reassuring words of John today. Read 1 John 5:18-20.

PERSONAL REFLECTION: What stood out to you? Don't think too hard. Write whatever comes to mind.

We do not continue to sin -

What three things does John say "we know"?

1. *any one born of God does not continue to sin*

2. *We are children of God*

3. *Son of God has come - gives us understanding*

Because I feel the perpetual need to organize John, let's lay each of these out like three tidy wicker baskets we can arrange his thoughts into.

Tidy Wicker Basket One (v. 18)

When John says that those born of God do not sin (or continue to sin), he is speaking of those who persist in the sins he's pointed out in his epistle. This is part of our assurance as believers: we don't need to worry about having committed the deadly sins John talked about yesterday, because we're born of God.

PERSONAL REFLECTION: Can you think of a time when you were struggling with a certain sin but the Holy Spirit wouldn't allow you to continue in that sin? How did the Holy Spirit intervene and convict you? What did it feel like? How did He rescue you?

This idea of recklessly persisting in sin without regard to the conviction of the Holy Spirit is terrifying. While I've never loved discipline in the present moment or forsaking sins that are often pleasurable, I wouldn't trade the Lord weighing on my conscience like a boulder for anything in the world. I'm also grateful for the times He intervened and rescued me from my sin even when I ignored His conviction. He does that too and it's just pure grace.

> John gives us a reason for why those born of God won't live their lives in reckless, prolonged, unrepentant sin. What reason does he give?
>
> ☑ Jesus keeps us.   ❑ Jesus loves us.
> ❑ Jesus forgives us.   ❑ Jesus anoints us.

We've seen this word several times in John's letter. The word *keep* in the Greek is *terei* and means *to attend to carefully, take care of, to guard, to keep one in the state in which he is*. Here's what I'm loving about this: So far we've only seen this word as it relates to something we do, such as keeping God's Word or His commands. But in this case, it's Jesus who is doing the keeping and we're the ones He's keeping! This is stunning imagery and truth. It's more than I can even grasp.

I want you to see another passage where God does the keeping. See Jesus' words in John 17:11. Your translation may use a different English word than *keep* here, but it's the same Greek word *terei*.   *Remain*

> **PERSONAL REFLECTION:** Based on the definition of *terei*, what means the most to you about the reality that Jesus keeps you?

John also says that when we're born of God, the Evil One cannot touch us. This doesn't mean we won't have dangers, suffer, or go through hardship, but it absolutely means we cannot be taken from the possession of the Father. (See Rom. 8:35-39 about how nothing can separate us from the love of God.)

Tidy Wicker Basket Two (v. 19)

> **PERSONAL TAKE:** Why do you think John inserts—right here—that we know we're children of God while the whole world is under the sway of the Evil One?

John leaves no middle ground here. Either we're of God or we're languishing under the Evil One. Culturally this is not a progressive idea in any way. We don't like to make demarcations these days, at least not in the neighborhood where I live. But John snaps me back to the reality that there really are two kingdoms—light and dark—and I need to live more urgently for the sake of those who are literally lying helpless under the control of the Evil One. The term here is *to lie,* as in how baby Jesus lay in a manger.

While this is a stark verse, I adore what John Stott points out: The term "whole world" is only used twice by John in this letter, here and in 1 John 2:2 where John says that Jesus Christ is the propitiation for the whole world.[8] So the whole world that lies under the control of the Evil One is not beyond the reach of the One who rescues us. We need to be proactive about telling the good news.

Tidy Wicker Basket Three (v. 20)

PERSONAL REFLECTION: What truth from this verse do you treasure the most and why?

So we might know ...

This is the only time in any of John's writings where he uses the word *understanding.* He uses the word *know* like it's going out of style, as my mom would say. But his sole use of *understanding* hits me in a timely way. If there's one idea that has seeped its way into mainstream culture and now into the church, it's that you can't know much of anything spiritually because everyone's understanding of Scripture is up for interpretation.

Theological and moral tenets of the Christian faith that have been accepted as truth since the inception of the church are now up for grabs. I want to be respected and liked by my community, but at times I feel dismissed because I still hold to this "narrow" thinking. My belief that God has a moral claim on our lives and that He gave us His Word and His Holy Spirit—so we could actually know and understand some things—is often looked upon as confining and antiquated. As a result I often feel misunderstood and at times lonely.

What's encouraging—and discouraging at the same time—is only 70 years after Christ's ascension John was dealing with similar mindsets. But how beautiful that here John contends Jesus has come and He has given us understanding! The Son of God didn't come to give us a ridiculous faith void of any foundation or thoughtfulness. He didn't come to offer us something so vague that it has no practical affects on our lives.

What reason does John give for why Jesus gave us understanding?

So we might know him who is true.

I know it goes against every grain in our society, but don't believe the lie that you can't know or understand what you believe. I get it. I know it's avant garde to hold nebulous beliefs that are open ended and that allow for pretty much whatever is comfortable for you and the people around you. But the Christian faith is preciously more defined than that. And this is actually wonderful news.

PERSONAL RESPONSE: Since the understanding Jesus came to give is all about us being able to know Him, I encourage you to read Ephesians 1:17-18 aloud as a prayer, asking that God would open the eyes of your understanding. Some translations may use the phrase "eyes of your heart." Take some time to ask Him for this. I believe the Lord loves answering this prayer. *So you may know Him better -*

We're almost to the end of 1 John. I'm not sure the study of any book has changed or challenged me more than this one. I think it's because I've been forced to marinate in so many theological truths I've casually understood in my head, but hadn't taken the time—or had the belief— to let penetrate into my daily life.

Even the way John ends verse 20 by saying that we're actually in God and in His Son Jesus Christ is a profound, life changing truth if we can bring ourselves to believe it. More accurately, if we will ask God for the grace to understand so we can believe it.

In a world that says there's not much you can know, John says there are at least three things you can. One being Jesus Himself and nothing on earth could be better. *See page 144*

KEEP YOURSELVES FROM IDOLS

It just wouldn't be right if John ended his letter in a standard sort of way. That would be much too … well, standard, for him. While teaching this book at my home church my friend April said to me on the last night of our study—approximately two minutes before I stood up to teach—"I hope John ends on an upbeat note." This really depends on your definition of *upbeat*. So without further ado, I'd love for you to read the very last sentence of 1 John, verse 5:21.

> **PERSONAL TAKE:** Keeping John's full epistle in mind, why do you think he chose to end his letter with this particular charge?

Part of what I've come to love about John and this letter—as well as what has made me want to run screaming through the streets—is that John doesn't always write what you'd expect. And his farewell is no different. Most translations use only six words in making up this concluding verse but they're as rich and personally relevant as they can be. If we will actually do what he says here, there's no telling where God will take us.

> First of all, what phrase does John use to address his readers for the seventh and final time, and how does it warm your heart?
>
> *Keep yourselves from idols —*
>
> What concluding directive does John give?

Scholars aren't clear as to why John would bring up idols from seemingly out of nowhere, nor are they clear on what type of idols he's referring. The good news is that the Bible as a whole speaks to this topic from Exodus to Revelation so the concept is fully accessible to us. The main two questions are: 1) What prompted John to address idolatry at the close of his letter? 2) Is he speaking broadly to the subject or were there specific threats of idol worship during the time of his writing?

Most likely John wrote his letter while living in Ephesus. Acts gives us a clear picture of the idol worship prevalent in that region at the time.

What types of gods were the people of Ephesus worshipping? Read
Acts 17:29-30; 19:23-28.

Another possibility is the general influence of the Roman Empire at the
time, which was decorated by pagan gods (see Rom. 1:23, 1 Cor. 8:4-6,
1 Thess. 1:9). John may also have had in mind idols of the heart which
Ezekiel 14:4 refers to.

To what actions does Paul link idolatry? Read Colossians 3:5.

Sexual immorality   evil desires
impurity   greed.
Lust

As far as our Western culture is concerned we're not as known for our
worship of stone or wooden statues, but that doesn't mean we don't
have an idolatry problem. I love this quote from Ken Sande: "[An idol] is
something other than God that we set our heart on, that motivates us,
that masters and rules us, or that we trust, fear or serve … An idol can
also be referred to as a false god or a functional god."[9]

PERSONAL REFLECTION: Given this definition, what relationships,
behavior, or pleasures have you set your heart on that have taken
the place of God in your life?

While any form of idolatry leads us away from the heart of God,
understanding this issue in the context of John's day is important.
Keeping the context of 1 John in mind we're aware by now that the
biggest issue John was dealing with were those who denied the true
God revealed in Jesus.

While any form of idolatry ultimately leads us away from the heart of
God, I'm particularly interested in how John was viewing this issue during
his day. The crisis of troubling distortions about Jesus and the false
gospel that had infiltrated his community was a significant reason for
John's writing. I really want to get into John's head about this because of
the distortions of biblical truth I see permeating the society in which we
currently live. Especially the distortions about Jesus.

PERSONAL REFLECTION: The type of false gods John may have had in mind were the heretical images of God being perpetrated by the antichrists. Can you think of any ways our culture has twisted the Jesus of the Bible into an idol it tries to manipulate or control? Respond in the margin.

One way I see this happening is how people often describe Jesus as merely a kind man who went around helping people. A woman I deeply respect in ministry commented that the church at large is in danger of forgetting that while Jesus is indeed love, He is also God and King. He should have authority over every aspect of our lives. It's so easy to slip into the mindset that Jesus is a tenderhearted religious figure we can get to sign off on any of our decisions or desires, so long as we tack Him onto our lives like a pin on our lapels. In light of this, John implores us to keep ourselves from false gods (the Greek reads with great urgency).

Your translation may say *keep yourselves from idols* while others say *guard*. To better understand John's usage we'll turn to a few other passages that use this exact term.

In the verses below, what was being guarded, and who was doing the guarding?

Luke 2:8
what - Sheep   Who - Shepherds .

Acts 12:4-5   Peter
what - ~~Jesus~~   Who - 4 squads - 4 soldiers = 16

1 Timothy 6:20
what - "has been entrusted to her care - Who Timothy

By telling us to guard ourselves from idols, John is leaving us with a personal responsibility. Even though God is faithful to keep us (see 1 John 5:18), we have some keeping to do as well.

PERSONAL REFLECTION: Like the shepherds in Luke guarded their flocks through midnight's darkness, the soldiers guarded Peter in prison, and Timothy kept what had been entrusted to his care, in what ways do you specifically guard yourself against idols?

I am so personally connected to this topic that it made up the theme of my first Bible study, *No Other Gods*. In a nutshell, even though I was a believer in Jesus, I found myself in a continual state of joyless, miserable, discontented, anxious living. I couldn't for the life of me figure out what my problem was. I was in Bible study, attending church, even leading worship. And then one day when I was out on a run (or in my case, a jog), the Lord revealed the core of my misery to me. The Holy Spirit spoke in my heart as clear as I know His voice. "No other gods," He said.

> Briefly turn to Exodus 20:1-3. What had the Lord done for Israel and what did He require of them?
>
> *Out of Egypt — No other Gods . . .*

I'll never tire of the fact that the Lord said to the Israelites, "I am the LORD *your* God." Don't ever believe the lie that God is an impersonal, distant deity who's removed from your heart's longings. He is your God, indeed. Not only is He your God but through Jesus He's delivered you from your bondage. John reminds us that He is so intimately involved that He loved us first and offered Himself as an atonement for our sins. Because of His immense love and His overwhelming greatness, we simply have no room or time for the false gods that pull our attention away from Him.

The Lord began to reveal to me that my life had become overcrowded with the false gods, including relationships I had put far too much emphasis on, a career in music I was looking to fulfill me, notoriety and success I thought would bring me meaning. All of these and more were differing versions of idolatry to which I was looking for life.

> **PERSONAL RESPONSE:** Is the Holy Spirit bringing to mind any false gods in your life? Is He prompting you to guard yourself? I can't encourage you enough to write out a prayer forsaking whatever that idol is. Be obedient. Don't let any desire, pleasure, behavior, or belief get in the way of your relationship with the one true God. *Your* God. Write your prayer in the margin.

I'd always known Jesus brought life in the far off, eternal sense, but I had no idea the life He wanted to bring me life in the here and now. I didn't realize how much my idols were substituting for that real life. I can't say that the road to freedom has been easy. In fact, forsaking some of those idols made up some of the most painful years of my life. But I wouldn't trade the freedom, peace and intimacy I now have with Jesus for one second of one moment with those false gods. I am forever indebted to the Lord for delivering me from them. And though the Lord was faithful to keep me (see 1 John 5:18), I had to do some keeping as well. So do you. We have to actively guard ourselves from idols. But nothing is more worth it. "Avoid the sham, John warns, and keep to the genuine of which I have spoken."[10]

COCONUT CHICKEN

FROM THE KITCHEN OF ANDREA KORNBLUE

LifeWay ran a recipe contest and these were the winners we chose both for their simplicity and flavor. Also, my feeling is you can never know too many ways to serve up chicken. The coconut, mustard, curry and honey dress up the average chicken breast. Serve with rice and mint peas and you have yourself an easy and impressive meal. And who doesn't love a great dessert!

RECIPE INGREDIENT LIST

3 Chicken Breasts or Chicken Tenders
  (we use organic)
6 TBS Coconut Oil
1/3 cup Local Honey
1 TBS Dijon Mustard
1 TBS Curry Powder
1/2 Cup Unsweetened Shredded Coconut

Carefully wash chicken and pat dry.
Mix the coconut oil, honey, dijon and curry powder. Dip the chicken pieces in the mix and place in a shallow casserole dish.

Bake at 325* for 30 minutes.

Sprinkle chicken with coconut and bake another 15 minutes until coconut is golden brown.
Enjoy!

PEANUT BUTTER AND BISCOFF NO BAKE COOKIES

FROM THE KITCHEN OF RUTH HARTUNIAN-ALUMBAUGH

RECIPE INGREDIENT LIST

- 2 cups sugar
- 4 T. cocoa
- 1 stick butter
- 1/2 cup milk
- 1/2 cup peanut butter (or almond or cashew or other butter)
- 1/2 cup Biscoff spread or your favorite brand cookie spread (creamy or crunchy, either will do)
- 1 T. vanilla
- 3 cups oatmeal (or other "flake" such as amaranth, etc.)
- waxed paper

RECIPE INSTRUCTIONS

In heavy saucepan, bring the first four ingredients to a boil. After one minute of boiling, add the nut butter and spread, vanilla and oatmeal. Drop mixture by teaspoonfuls on wax paper or spread into a pan lined in aluminum foil. Let cool until hard. Store cookies in airtight container. Cut pan cookies to shape you wish and store in airtight container.

They won't last long!

THIS BEAUTIFUL BRIDE

We're not done yet. I know it feels a little like we're done but don't relax into that thought. We still have 2 and 3 John ahead of us, two of the most overlooked books in the New Testament. You are going to love them. 2 John is addressed specifically to one church in the Johannine community and 3 John narrows even further to one individual. These two tiny letters show us a slice of early church life and remind us that the Lord is still working in this group of flawed Christ followers He calls His bride.

I am the firstborn of four and was born a year after my Dad started a church in Reston, VA where he still faithfully pastors and where my Mom continues to serve her kids and grandkids, her church family, and a slew of casseroles. I'm reminded of my heritage at the most unusual times, like when I flew home a couple years ago to visit my newborn niece, Harper, and discovered a life-size shepherd's staff leaning against the corner of the guest bedroom. This would be considered a "normal" piece in an evangelical pastor's home, something my Mom has had to contend with over the years. She mostly wins but occasionally there's the shepherd's staff.

Growing up in a pastor's home was a world unto itself. What always felt run-of-the-mill to me I later realized was anything but. Among other, mostly wonderful, things growing up in our home meant a rich exposure to different parts of the world—missionaries staying at our home or my Dad off to another country to preach. He had a penchant for bringing home some of the oddest gifts known to humankind. The chocolate brown fur rug with a scary white cat in the middle of it, that didn't go with a thing in our house, for instance; I have no idea how he hauled that thing through security. Then there were the woven coasters he packed into his suitcase from Coachabamba, Bolivia as a "gift" to my mom and several other close friends in the ministry. They reeked to high heavens and I don't think they were ever used for anything other than us kids passing them around, doubled over in laughter because they smelled like doodie. After the coaster fiasco came a trip to Russia where my dad brought home to my mother a crystal statue of The Kremlin. Let's just say neither coasters nor Kremlin survived my parents' last move, which is saying a lot when you consider Cabbage Patch Dolls® made it out alive.

Some of the things we find funny or odd about the church is just church culture, which is actually different from the church itself. Shepherd's staffs, coasters, and crystal Kremlins aside, the church body is the greatest gift my parents ever gave me. The church has sustained me through deep depression, literally rescued me from sin that would have destroyed me, forged my character, and made me laugh until I couldn't breathe. Some of this was formal but most of it happened as we all went along in life.

When I was somewhere in the abyss of junior high I remember Mary Wolfe splitting open a two pound bible on her stairwell, offering a timely word to me and her daughter Shannon, one of my best friends growing up, about how to love those we found difficult. This was revolutionary stuff because you're not born considering how you can put others before yourself, and the whole of Junior High is like kryptonite to this way of thinking. Eric and Michelle Smith let us youth group kids terrorize their home on the weekends—once we nearly burned down the house with a late-night microwave popcorn bash gone awry. Though I didn't quite get it at the time, they were modeling the sacrifice and generous gift of hospitality, a trait they so naturally wore they may have offered it even beyond biblical recommendations. When I left home for the first time, Linda Mitchell, another of my best friend's moms, handwrote me a letter based on Isaiah 43:1-4. Her words comforted me with the truth of how God's presence carries us through rising waters and blazing fires. She tucked it in a gorgeous leather bag and sent me out the door to Nashville. I would reference that letter a hundred times over.

Because of the embrace of the church it pains me when I hear of so many leaving the church, especially young people, because if I hadn't had the church when I was young I just don't know where I'd be. And if I didn't have it now I would have no one with whom to share the life of Christ. And the life of Christ is a shared life. Now you may be thinking that when I say "church" that I mean Sunday morning services, and I do mean this in part. Sunday morning at my local church is a lighthouse for me, a place that helps me catch my bearings. Corporate worship and prayer and a solid message from the Bible from my pastor are bulwarks from the onslaught of what a week can bring. Sunday mornings are grounding. But when I say "church" I also mean the body of Christ at large. I mean the fellowship of believers that, John says at the top of 1 John, the incarnation of Jesus made possible. I'm talking about everyday communing over the shared life of Christ. We live in such an individualistic society where everyone is focused on his or her personal story. "Some of us are so westernized and individualized and evangelicalized that we have forgotten how much we really need each other."[1]

As we meditate this week on 2 and 3 John and reflect on the beautiful bride of Christ we will see it is not perfect. There are battles going on from within and without, those who seek to distort truth, who were running ahead of Christ's teachings, along with gossipers, slanderers, some who only care about being first. And as you read these letters, perhaps you will come across some painful realities that have specifically wounded you, causing you to isolate or detach. We are not a perfect institution, that is for sure, and John's letters affirm this. But the church is nothing less than Christ's bride. When loving in unity she is still the city on a hill, the only hope for the world, the best argument for a Messiah who came in the flesh. No matter how you've been hurt by the church or what must be healed in your heart, don't forsake her for anything; she is Christ's bride and you have much to offer her. And she, you.

VIEWER GUIDE

LOVE

#1 Obedience is built on trust and trust is vital to _____.

#2 Obedience is built on _____.

#3 Obedience is built on what God wants to _____.

GROUP DISCUSSION QUESTIONS:

What was the most impacting moment for you this week (in video or print study)?

In a culture of countless opinions regarding what love is, how has your definition of love either broadened or narrowed through this study?

Why do you suppose God sometimes demands painful or sacrificial obedience of His children? How have these experiences of obedience served as meaningful expressions of how we love God back?

How have you come to a better understanding of the "sin that leads to death"? (p. 142)

How has the Holy Spirit rescued you by refusing to let you continue in a specific sin? (p. 144)

TRUTH AND LOVE

"Most churches could function a whole lifetime without 2 John or 3 John in their Bibles and never miss their absence,"[2] said one encouraging scholar. He has a point. Even if we venture as far as 1 John, making it to 2 and 3 feels almost overachiever-ish. Plus, we feel this subconscious undercurrent that if we've gotten 1 John down, which is longer and more comprehensive than the others, and with the number one in the title, do we really need to bother with its tinier siblings?

I'm about to talk you into it.

First I am loving these brief little letters that would have fit perfectly on one piece of papyrus. Both 2 and 3 John narrow the focus from the church at large to one specific church in 2 John and to a specific individual in 3 John, so the whole feel turns more personal. We see how John's passion for truth and love plays out in real life circumstances during a real crisis. First John sheds light on 2 and 3, and 2 and 3 shed light on 1 John. I am so excited about these two letters. They may be short but they're not small. Read 2 John 1-3.

> In Hellenistic times the author of a letter identified himself at the top instead of signing off at the end. Based on this information, how does John refer to himself and to whom is he writing?
>
> *The Elder*
>
> John loves the recipients of this letter in the _*Truth*_ (v. 1).
>
> In verse 3, John promises his readers three blessings that will be with them. What are they? (Note, this is the first time we've seen these words used together in John's writings.)
>
> *Grace*
> *mercy*
> *Peace*

You might remember that John didn't identify himself at all in 1 John, but in both 2 and 3 John he goes by *the elder*. This literally means *old man*, which is so endearing I can hardly take it. I have grown to love John as an elderly, wise, passionate, protective father who I wish was still living, so I could ask him some questions. The title also implies an apostolic authority John would have held over this particular community, the elect lady, and

While debate exists, many scholars give substantial argument for John as the author of 2 and 3 John.

her children. While some believe the elect lady was an individual it appears most scholars believe this title represents a single house church that was part of the Johannine community. As well, it's possible that John remained vague in his salutations if the letter were to fall into the wrong hands, since Roman authorities would have frowned upon this kind of letter.[3]

> **PERSONAL TAKE:** In verse 2 John says that the truth lives in us and will be with us forever. How would you describe the difference between knowing truth and having it literally dwell inside you?

Many of the people I've met along the way, primarily outside of Christianity, tend to either reject the idea of absolute truth or they're satisfied only by empirical truth that can be proved by science and reason. But John reveals another facet of truth altogether—that Jesus' truth actually dwells (we know this word well now) inside us. This gives me a confidence I don't naturally possess on my own. I'm not much of a debater and when I'm in a position to discuss the truths of Christianity with an unbeliever, I rarely feel adequate. But the truth that dwells in me, which I think is part of the anointing we studied on Week 3, Day 3, thrives independently of me having all the right answers or intellectual arguments. I'm much more at ease when I remember that God is pleased to use the truth that lives inside me.

> What two foundational ingredients does John mention at the end of verse 3? _Truth_ and _Love_

You can't have love without truth and you can't have truth without love. An example of the former would be the reams of television and movies portraying "love" stories that emerge from affairs, or are defined by what the Bible deems as sexually immoral. The latter might look like an angry preacher pounding on his Bible about a moral truth, while being arrogant, unteachable, and ultimately unloving.

I have sometimes treated people in ways that looked like love when really I was just allowing their harmful behavior to go unchallenged because I was too afraid to speak the truth (love not according to truth). At other times I've been too hard on people, impatient, or judgmental when they fell short of the truth (truth not according to love).

PERSONAL REFLECTION: Briefly describe a situation when you:

1. Acted toward another person in truth but realized you needed to bring the love.

2. Acted toward another person in love but realized it was time to bring the truth.

Continue reading verses 4-6. What was John "overjoyed" to find in this body of believers?

This is so much more than saying you believe in Jesus or that you try to live a moral life. Walking in the truth, or living in truth revealed in Jesus Christ affects everything: our attitudes, flavor of conversations, sexual behavior, use of money and time, tone of our voices, what we watch and listen to, the words we speak. Truth lays down the path on which God calls us to walk.

PERSONAL REFLECTION: As the spiritual father of this body of believers, John says that he was overjoyed to find some who were walking in the truth. In what ways do you experience the same kind of joy when you see your own children, spouse, nieces or nephews, or those you disciple taking steps on the path of truth?

I am deeply moved that, after John's strong emphasis on the truth command, he quickly pulls the love command back into the equation. This means a great deal to me because I grew up learning a lot about truth sometimes in a vacuum void of love. One of the big "truth preachers" of my childhood was convicted years later of having been abusive to the females on his staff. Truth without love is disastrous, and in some ways no truth at all. John knew this well.

Look back at 1 John 3:23. How does this verse combine both the truth and love command that John speaks of in 2 John 4-5?

Truth lays down the path on which God calls us to walk.

In verse 6 John spells out a distinctive of love. Complete the sentence: "And this is love…

We wAlk in obedience to his Commands

We've already considered how closely John tied obeying God's commands to loving God (see John 15:10; 1 John 3:23). But in 2 John 5-6 we discover that obeying His commands also demonstrates our love for others.

> **PERSONAL TAKE:** Why do you think our loving others is invariably tied to our obeying God's commands?

I don't mean to harp on culture. I love culture and what emerges from it: thoughtful movies, seasonal cuisine, art, music, expression, flair. But culture tends to offer a thin reflection of love. It's often based on feeling, passion, lust, fluctuating desire, personal gain, or sex. John attaching love to living according to God's commands is truly novel.

> **PERSONAL RESPONSE:** How might a specific relationship in your life look different if you loved that person by obeying a command of God you're currently neglecting?

In verses 4 and 6 John tells us to walk in two things. One more time—what are they?

Truth & Love

We tend to view these two virtues as being at odds with one another. I'll hear one crowd bellow from a corner of social media, "This 'certain group' isn't living according to the truth. They're damned and condemned." While another says, "The Bible is anti-love with all its rules and exclusive claims on truth." But John's opening to this very special congregation sews truth and love together as if they simply can't be worn apart. Truth and love aren't enemies. They're not mutually exclusive. In fact, John says it's because of the truth that he loves. Truth defines love and love expresses truth.

Truth defines love and love expresses truth.

> **PERSONAL RESPONSE:** We integrate truth and love in real life when we're obedient to God's commands. Name one area of your life where God is requesting obedience. Make a commitment to obey and watch how love for others mysteriously springs forth.

The true revelation of today's text is that we can only love others to the extent that we're obeying God. I find it fascinating that John essentially says, "You want to love others? Obey God's commands." What an interesting truth that I've watched play out in my life over and over. When I couldn't figure out how to love certain people in my life, I could usually point to a truth I was neglecting.

Lastly, I love that the command to walk in love is just that, a command. Jesus wouldn't have given us the love command if He hadn't made walking in it possible. Ask the Lord to give you the capacity to love, to have immeasurable compassion, sweet affection, and a deep well of grace. Amen.

DAY 2
DON'T RUN AHEAD

My youngest sister, Katie, has been newly appreciating the work of the Holy Spirit in her prayers, listening intently to His voice. She'd just asked the Lord to speak to her about the purpose of her life, even asking Him to send another person to confirm it. In that moment the doorbell rang. "I'm telling you," Katie said to me on the phone, all younger-sister intense, "the doorbell rang THAT MINUTE." She opened the door to two women who said, "God has sent us to reveal to you your life's purpose." Then they handed her a pamphlet that had an image on the front that was uniquely meaningful to Katie and told her something specifically related to what God has put on her heart for the poor. After a short dialogue Katie found out that they were members of a cult. She started shaking. They seemed like a direct answer to prayer and yet their beliefs about Jesus were blatantly contrary to what John tells us about Him and what Jesus declared about Himself.

When Katie told me this story I thought about what we've already studied in 1 John 4:1-6 about testing and recognizing the spirit of truth and the spirit of deceit. Even though these women came speaking in an eerily timely and specifically meaningful way to my sister, they did not pass John's test: believing that Jesus came in the flesh as the Son of God, the only atoning sacrifice for our sins. I believe the Enemy came to Katie's doorstep masquerading as an angel of light, trying to deceive her. But I also believe God used that encounter to sharpen Katie's discernment. Today, John is going to tell us to watch out (literally, watch ourselves) because the spirit of the antichrist is all around us. Sometimes in the most subtle and alluring of ways.

Read 2 John 7-9. How does John describe the deceivers in the world?
- ☑ They've gone out into it.
- ❏ They're hiding under bushes.
- ❏ They're huddled together.
- ❏ They've removed themselves from it.

Check the true statement:
- ❏ In the world there are a small number of deceivers.
- ☑ In the world there are many deceivers.

What does John tell us to specifically watch out for?

those who do not acknowledge Jesus as coming in the flesh —

What is the positive part of his warning?

You may be rewarded fully —

Being a Christian was not easy during the days of John. In his lifetime his dear friend Peter and his brother James had both been martyred for their faith. The Roman hostility to the spreading of Christianity was severe. All three of John's letters testify that significant opposition was coming against the church from the secessionists and those who claimed enlightenment apart from the orthodox teachings of Jesus. So you can hear John's passion when he says, don't lose what you've worked so hard for! Make sure you receive your full reward. Note: "The thought should not be confused with attempts to gain justification by works."[4] In other words, working hard doesn't gain us salvation.

PERSONAL TAKE: Give an illustration of what it may look like to throw away what you've worked for. I'll give you a couple to get you going: A twelve-year marriage that gets tossed away by an affair, or eight months of sobriety that is broken by a night of binge drinking.

PERSONAL REFLECTION: Based on what you know about the circumstances of John's era and the reading from today's text, what do you think his readers stood to lose?

In verse 9 John warns us about everyone who "runs ahead" or "beyond" by not continuing in the teachings of Christ. I really liked one commentator's translation: everyone who "innovates."[5] These particular deceivers were claiming a more enlightened way, a special *gnosis* superior to the antiquated beliefs of orthodox Christianity.

PERSONAL REFLECTION: What have you seen on television, read about, or heard in conversation that boasts a more progressive, enlightened belief system than Christianity?

Once again John offers a double-sided statement including a warning and a blessing—this is his specialty. We love him for these.

What do those who run ahead of Christ's teaching not have?

God

What do those who remain in Christ's teachings have?

have both the Father & Son

Growing up in the D.C. area I was surrounded by as many educated intellectuals as there are singers and mandolin players in Nashville. I found this stimulating, even if I regularly felt out of my league. We touched on this earlier, but the problem is when education and intellectualism become the supreme god or ultimate goal. John Stott said that the people of John's day "had advanced so far that they had even left God behind them!"[6]

Read 1 Corinthians 1:17-31.

This passage is a bit lengthy, but give yourself to its message. It's so rich especially for the days we're living in.

According to Paul, why is man's wisdom not the ultimate authority? Briefly note as many reasons as you can find.

God will destroy man's wisdom
through man's wisdom the world did not know Him

I can't help but notice how many people claim God but don't want anything to do with Jesus. More and more this is my experience with people I meet in social or business settings: You can talk about God, but it's harder to bring the name of Jesus into the conversation.

According to 2 John 9, it is impossible to forsake the teachings of Jesus while also claiming God. Because this is a potentially offensive message, we sometimes speak in vague terms about God.

PERSONAL RESPONSE: Are you willing to kindly and boldly speak specifically about Jesus in your social and work environments? If so, give a couple examples of how and where you can naturally do this.

Let's finish up the letter by reading 2 John 10-13.

Verse 10 is somewhat controversial because of several other verses in Scripture that tell us to practice hospitality. (Here are a few: Titus 1:8, Heb. 13:2, 1 Pet. 4:8-10.) Also, we are told to bless those who curse us (see Rom. 12:14). So why would John give such a strong, seemingly contradictory warning here? First it's important to note that the word *house* here implies the home that the church was meeting in. So, John is really talking about a church service in this instance. He's also speaking specifically in regard to those who came "not as a casual visitor but as an official teacher" of false doctrine.[7] Remember the church was truly under attack at this time. As well, John was specifically talking about those who had rejected the incarnation of Jesus. This wasn't about separating from people who you merely disagreed with over a side issue.

When I look at verse 10, I'm thankful for the caution John brings. Our homes and our places of worship are sacred spaces we are responsible for. Our pulpits should be places where Jesus' truth is proclaimed, our homes where the peace of His Spirit reigns. At the very same time, Jesus clearly set a precedent for us to reach out to the sinner, clothe the wounded Samaritans (the religious and social outcasts), offer gracious and sacrificial hospitality. I believe it requires sensitivity to the Holy Spirit to know whom we're to embrace and whom we're to protect ourselves from. The Lord has surprised me at times by asking me to reach out to people in situations I wouldn't have thought was a good idea. Other times, He has made it abundantly clear with whom I was to break ties.

PERSONAL RESPONSE: Choose one of the options:
Has the Lord spoken to you about a toxic situation you are no longer supposed to "welcome into your house"? If so, describe what obedience looks like.

Is the Lord asking you to reach out with the love of Jesus to someone you've held a prejudice or judgment toward? If so, describe how you are willing to do this.*

John couldn't have had any idea how profound his closing remarks in verse 12 would prove to be in the twenty-first century. In our day of text messages and social media, I long with all my heart to see people face to face. John gives the reason he wants to see them face to face: "so that our joy may be complete"!

PERSONAL RESPONSE: Who do you need to see face to face? Ask the Holy Spirit to bring someone to mind who needs you or whom you may need. It may require airfare, a road trip, or a simple dinner reservation. Commit to it here.

The urgent times John was living in seem less and less different from today. This is somewhat strange for me to write because in many respects I grew up in a relatively Christian nation. Even in the progressive D.C. area, going to public school with children whose parents had biblical morals, who went to church, and claimed Jesus, at least in a general way, was relatively normal. This is not altogether vanished but I am spending my thirties in an increasingly secular society, one in which having a belief in God does not necessarily mean holding to the teachings of Jesus (2 John 9). I believe we have some formidable times ahead of us, but we won't be facing them alone. Whoever has Jesus has the Father. And the joy of fellowship with the saints. Keep pressing into the teachings of Christ and the fellowship of the church. A great reward awaits you.

*If the situation requires endorsing a teacher who rejects the teachings of Jesus in a way that supports his or her false beliefs, John is clear that this would be to share in the wickedness of his or her work. But loving, evangelizing, and blessing our enemies are always encouraged.

A PERSONAL NOTE

I love letters. I'm a words-of-affirmation person, as my mom calls me. A gift card is handy, a new sweater warm, but words are the best. Especially from someone I love or look up to. So it suits my nature that the last letter we're going to study of John's is addressed to a single individual, written on a single piece of papyrus with the ink of John's pen. The personal touch comes at the perfect time as our study begins to draw to a close.

> Read 3 John 1-8. What, if anything, feels different to you about this letter as compared with 1 or 2 John? (Try to go beyond that it's addressed to a single individual.)

> What themes or words are similar to 1 and 2 John?
>
> *Truth*.

The name Gaius means *rejoicing* and was a common Roman name of the time. Three other men named Gaius are mentioned in the New Testament but none can be unequivocally tied to the Gaius of 3 John.

> Though we're not exactly sure who Gaius is, what do we know about him so far? Give as many details and characteristics—even implications—as you can find.

> Skim through today's reading once more, this time focusing on John's affection for Gaius. After reading the text, note one or more younger people for whom you have this type of affection. If you can't think of anyone, take a moment to ask the Lord to give you "children" or younger sisters in the faith.

Cheering and supporting those coming behind us is vital to our faith and the health of the church. Sometimes it's hard for me to pour into people younger than I am because of my own insecurities. I wonder if I'm out of touch, too "Bible girl," or too single to relate. I pick my own lettuce and stare at my asparagus plants—See? I have problems. And this is not to mention the time that loving others requires. We wonder if we have the space to meet with the person who wants to have coffee. The young mother who needs parenting advice from an older mom. The newly-married bride whose marriage is already rocky. The teenager who admires the fact that we just graduated college and still love the Lord. We all have someone we can give ourselves to and the vitality of the church depends on it. If these relationships are lacking in our lives, typically it's not because these younger women in the faith don't exist but because we haven't reached out to them.

> **PERSONAL REFLECTION:** What keeps you from reaching out to and loving a "Gaius" in your life? Ask the Holy Spirit to reveal the obstacles that hold you back. Respond in the margin.

John preached about love in his first and second letters and now he's showing us what love looks like as he pours into his beloved Gaius. I love the way John loves.

> John praises Gaius's spiritual state but also mentions two other prayers for him. What are they in verse 2?
>
> *Enjoy good health*
> *all may go well to you —*

Sometimes Christians are accused of only caring for a person's spiritual condition, disregarding their physical needs, health, or emotional distress. I love how John is about the whole person of Gaius, mentioning his physical health as well as a blessing that he "be led along a good road" of success.[8] As Charles Spurgeon once said, "If you give a man the gospel, wrap it in a sandwich. And if you give a man a sandwich, wrap it in the gospel."[9] We need to be about all the needs of a person.

> **PERSONAL TAKE:** How does John's care for Gaius's entire being encourage and challenge you to care for the whole of people?

> In verse 3 John mentions a group of brothers and sisters in the faith who had traveled to see Gaius. What did they report about him and how did this make John feel?
>
> *their faithfulness — continue to WALK in the truth — John feels Joy —*

These brothers and sisters were most likely itinerant ministers who had come out of John's church and had traveled to see Gaius and the church he belonged to. It's possible they had gone to Gaius's fellowship to encourage them in the tenets of the Christian faith in light of the deception that was spreading in the church. John reveals how delighted he was to hear that Gaius was walking in the truth. The HCSB defines the biblical term *walking* as *a way of life or behavior*.[10] This implies that Gaius's basic way of life was in accordance with God's truth as revealed in Jesus.

Walking in the truth doesn't mean a life of perfection but it does mean you're pointed in the direction of Christ. One of the challenges of today is that the plumb line of truth is being replaced with a sea of wavering opinions. Hear me—I'm not saying that everything is always black and white or cut and dried. If you hung out with me in my head you'd know I live with a hundred questions and that I don't view every decision as simply right or wrong. But the more I immerse myself in Scripture, prayer, and fellowship, the more clearly the way of Jesus' truth emerges.

> **PERSONAL REFLECTION:** Pretend you're living during the time of John. You look up to him a great deal, and you find out he's sending a group of friends to see how you're doing. (These are not judgmental Christians coming to stake you out in your sin.) How would they find you in this moment? Are you walking in the truth? Compromising? On the brink of denying Jesus? Take some time to confess whatever areas of your life are keeping you from walking in the truth. Remember you have an Advocate in Jesus who delights to restore and purify you (see 1 John 2:1-2).
>
> Gaius not only walked in the truth, but he showed hospitality to this group of brothers and sisters in the faith. This was especially significant because these people were:
>
> ❑ dear friends ❑ musicians
> ❑ celebrities ❑ strangers

Perhaps one of my strongest childhood memories from growing up in the church was the common bond I shared with believers in Jesus from all over the world. My parents hosted quite a few families from other countries or missionaries who were visiting on furlough. The Fiores from Italy always brought us kids Italian chocolate and were never without a ladies' leather boot that served as a handy map of Italy. I have fond memories of the way we had instant fellowship with those we had never met before, some who turned into lifelong friends.

John described these brothers and sisters as those who set out for the sake of the ___*Name*___ (v. 7).

While the face of global and local missions has changed over the years we can still support those on the front lines of sharing the good news of Jesus at home or abroad. We can offer a room in our homes to visiting missionaries, give monthly support, commit to pray, volunteer a Saturday out of the month, take a short-term mission trip, take your pastor out to dinner. (Whenever I go to Chicago I bring my pastor back caramel corn. I don't know if this counts.) The point is, we all have a part in the church. Some are called to go and some are called to stay. But if you're called to stay you're also called to help support those who go. We're a team.

PERSONAL RESPONSE: Do you know anyone who's laboring for the gospel and who could use your support? If you sense the Lord leading, will you commit to this person (or family) in a tangible way? If so, write down what you're being led to do. If you have fears, write them out before the Lord.

John encourages us to show hospitality and support for those laboring in the gospel. What does he say we will be partners or coworkers in according to verse 8?

Work together for the truth.

My heart is full as I write. I think of my friends J.Mac and Julie Brown who took me in for over a year when I was traveling between Virginia and Nashville. I was a friend of a friend of a friend whom they'd never laid eyes on before offering me a room in their home. This offering turned into way more nights and meals and me needing things—like J.Mac to replace the spark plugs in my barely-running Jeep—than they could have possibly anticipated. Have I mentioned that they had three children at the time with a fourth who came during one of my stays? The Browns' hospitality was truly remarkable, and it wasn't even like I could claim "laborer of the truth" like the brothers in John's day. I'll forever be grateful to them for giving me a place to get my feet on the ground. My prayer is that I would do the same for someone who needed me in a similar way.

As we consider the privilege we have to partner in the work of the truth, I would say this: If you're not concretely involved in supporting an individual who's given his or her life to the ministry, I can't encourage you enough to make this a priority. Not that we do it for our own glory—that would be to miss the point—but how wonderful it was for Gaius to hear these words from John: "They have told the church about your love." (3 John 6). What more beautiful words could be said of us?

WHOEVER LEADS MUST SERVE

John has been called the apostle of love but he is also a "broker of fellowship," a title I couldn't be fonder of.[11] In John's writings you feel his passion for the communion of believers with God and with one another. Because John feels so strongly about whole and healthy relationships bound in Christ, when they are compromised he gets feisty. I understand this. One of the most difficult parts of the Christian life for me has been when relationships are broken, don't go the way I'd hoped, or someone hinders another from walking in the truth. We grieve because as Christians this is not the way things are supposed to go. I wish I could offer you a tidier example of how the church in John's day was doing, but one of the things I love about Scripture is that it tells it like it is.

Read 3 John 9-14.

For ease of understanding, here's what may not be obvious at first glance: Gaius was most likely a member of the congregation that Diotrephes was trying to overtake. John had sent a letter to Gaius's church that evidently was disputed by Diotrephes (v. 9). It's possible the letter in question was 2 John, though we can't be sure. We'll get further into the issues with Diotrephes in a minute, but clearly he and John did not see eye to eye. Demetrius is briefly introduced as someone John trusted and very possibly was the courier of the letter John had sent.

> Based on what we're given in verses 9-10, what were Diotrephes's offenses? *Love of Self - wants to be first Will have nothing to do ō others -*
>
> **PERSONAL REFLECTION:** I kind of hate to put it this way for Diotrephes's sake, but out of all his flaws you noted, with which do you struggle most?

We're not sure if John's main issue with Diotrephes was doctrinal or organizational (how the church was being run) or both, but one thing is clear: Diotrephes loved to have first place among the people. Just writing that makes me nervous because the temptation—even in Christian work—to be famous, idolized, a best seller, have the most followers,

When I read about
Diotrephes desiring to be
first, I have to examine my
own heart, because who
doesn't have this in them?

is powerful. If you're a mom, your passion for your children to succeed can turn into a Facebook post that's a whole lot more about you than them. If you're a businesswoman, your desire to excel can morph into an insatiable hunger to be front and center. A healthy love for your husband or boyfriend can go wayward when you start needing that person to feed your self-esteem as the most enviable girl in the church or neighborhood. So when I read about Diotrephes desiring to be first, I have to examine my own heart, because who doesn't have this in them?

Based on something we know about John from his much younger years, I find his comments about Diotrephes wanting to be first ironic. Turn to Luke 22 and read verses 24-27.

What was the dispute over?
who was the greatest.
Jesus' response was simple: The one who is greatest should become like the youngest. And the one who rules or leads should be like the one who ___*Serves*___ .

Now, turn to Mark 10:35.

Who were the two people who wanted to be the greatest in Jesus' kingdom? ___*James*___ and ___*John*___ .

PERSONAL TAKE: Do you think John's earlier encounter with Jesus made John particularly sensitive to Diotrephes's pride? If so, why?

Whenever God sets us free from a particular sin or struggle we're extra sensitive to it in others. I don't even mean in a judgmental way, necessarily, but simply that we have eyes to see it. John knew about putting his personal ambition at the forefront. Decades later, when hearing of Diotrephes's lust for power and prestige in the congregation, I can't help but wonder if John wasn't transported back to the table a half a century earlier where Jesus looked him in the eye and said, "You want to lead? You must learn how to serve." From that moment on John spent a lifetime living that very truth. To lead in the church is to serve it.

PERSONAL REFLECTION: PART 1 In what area of your life are you desiring first place? Where are you clamoring to be the greatest, or right, or recognized?

PERSONAL REFLECTION: PART 2 How can you go from trying to be first to living out 1 John 3:16?

Lay down our Lives for our brothers.

For me, this comes into play every time I travel somewhere to speak. I continually pray that my motivation won't stem from personal ambition but out of a heart to serve. If I'm self-seeking I'll be concerned with how well I'm treated, how many people give me positive feedback, the number of women in the crowd. But if I'm propelled by Jesus' example to serve, then I'm looking for the person who looks lonely, left out, or hurting. I'll see each woman as an individual, not rushing her along but listening to her pains and joys.

One singer I recently worked with said from the stage, "I'm here until the last woman leaves." Kathy's heart to serve, pray over, and listen to every single woman is noteworthy and it's a great reminder that no matter what setting we're in—on stage, babysitting our niece and nephew, teaching a classroom, running a corporation—we're always to bear the heart of servants. Praise Jesus He's left us with this kind of example.

Back to our guy Diotrephes. I want to look at a couple more problems with his character. First Diotrephes was guilty of gossip, speaking maliciously about the church. I thought it was interesting that part of the original wording means *to prattle* or *speak absolute nonsense*. Sometimes a decent conversation can turn into fodder simply because we're bored or have run out of things to say. Even if we didn't start out with the intention to gossip we find ourselves blathering at the expense of others, commenting on things we should not be airing our opinions on. For me, it's when I'm all talked out that I have to watch out for gossip.

> **PERSONAL REFLECTION:** Think of someone you find it easy to gossip about. What positive remarks can you make about this person instead? If there's truly not much there—like, the only thing you can think of is that she painted her kitchen a nice color blue—can you at least commit to not participating in the detrimental conversation?

John also says Diotrephes prevented those who wanted to be part of John's community from doing so. Sometimes we draw our lines so strongly that if anyone disagrees with us we cut them off. Some things are worth distancing ourselves over (John was clear about these issues), but sometimes we can be so blinded in our self-righteous pursuit of power or protecting our spheres that we lop people off if they don't agree with every value or tenet we hold. Diotrephes went so far as to excommunicate those who didn't agree with him, while opposing the apostolic authority of John.

PERSONAL TAKE: How can you tell if you've drawn a line for the sake of Jesus or over your own pride, codependent relationships, desire to control or be right?

PERSONAL REFLECTION: Whom do you know who holds strong biblical convictions yet is also humble and welcoming to those who may have differing perspectives? Describe his or her characteristics.

It's possible that Diotrephes was trying to persuade Gaius to turn against John and the orthodox teachings of the early church. Re-read verses 11-14. What markers does John give Gaius to assure Gaius that John (and Demetrius whom he's sent) can be trusted?

Winsome, charismatic, and highly educated leaders vie for our attention. Sometimes we listen to a sermon, read a blog, or flip on an afternoon talk show, and we find ourselves as confused as ever. If you're Gaius, do you listen to John? Diotrephes? Demetrius? How do you know which way is the right way? Who's telling the truth? The beauty of this passage is that John—even with his unparalleled apostolic authority—goes back to a few touchstones.

How does John persuade Gaius that his teachings are trustworthy? (vv. 11-12)

Regardless of what Diotrephes was proclaiming, his behavior wasn't a reflection of his knowing God. He was malicious, defiant, and a divider of people. On the other hand, Demetrius (most likely the courier of the letter) had the endorsement of the Johannine church, he and John were known for their commitment to truth, their behavior was good, which indicated they knew the Lord. While John doesn't lay out an exact formula for us here, it's important that we test any new worldview or opinion with the unchanging truths of Scripture. We should also seek the opinions of godly people we respect. In John's case, he was able to tell Gaius that Demetrius had the favor and endorsement of the church. Lastly, the person's actions should be full of goodness, not evil.

> John signs off with words common to us but unique to his day. Whom does he tell Gaius to greet by name?

> Briefly look at Jesus' words to His disciples in John 15:15. How does Jesus refer to them?

I can't see how 3 John could end any better. The friends of John's church had sent their greetings to Gaius and now John asks Gaius to greet the friends in his church by name. The ESV (UK) translates it this way, "Greet the friends, every one of them." John's passion for community and friendship, even in trying situations like with Diotrephes, was the fuel that kept John going. He dealt with Diotrephes strongly but only because, as John Stott put it, "Self-love violates all relationships."[12]

The bond of friendship with Christ and with His church has always been at the forefront of John's heart. He began 1 John with the joy of fellowship and he ends 3 John with the joy of friendship. And what holds the Christlike bond of relationships together like that of truth manifested through love? There's no formula, no tidy or simplistic approach to ensure its safety. Only hearts like John's that beat with zeal for the truth of God's Word and overflow with compassion for the love expressed through Jesus.

Jerome recorded the tradition that when John was an old man he had to be carried into his church at Ephesus in the arms of his disciples. They would take him to the front where with barely the strength to speak, he'd say, "Little children, love one another!" The church members wearied of hearing him saying the same thing each week with nothing to add. "Master, why do you say this?" they asked. "It is the Lord's command" was John's reply, "and if this alone be done, it is enough."[13]

THE LIFE APPEARED

PERSONAL REFLECTION: What has been the single most significant concept of this study for you?

Ever since throwing myself into these letters the way a child finally inches off the high dive, I've been dog paddling in the deep end. You may feel the same way, having now peered into the mysteries of light and dark, cracked open words like *propitiation* and *chrisma,* tried to reconcile why, if the church is taught by the Holy Spirit, do so many believers disagree? If John tells us that we're all sinners why does he say that children of God don't sin? If Jesus Christ keeps us why do we have to be vigilant about making sure we stay abiding in Him?

I still have some questions and maybe you do too. Which is why I want to go back to the very beginning of 1 John and look at something we glossed over the first time around. Since John's whole premise for writing is based on "that which was from the beginning," I find it fitting to end our study with where it all began. This won't clear up every mystery and a few puzzle pieces may still be missing, but we'll have Christ with us. And His having come surpasses having all the answers.

Look back at 1 John 1:2.

Remind yourself from Week 1, Day 2 of what specific action the Word of Life took?

Proclaiming eternal life

Now turn to John's Gospel 1:14. What did the Word become?

flesh – dwelt among us –

Among whom did He make His dwelling?

us

You already know that what John declared here is the great doctrinal truth of the incarnation. Write out the definition of the word *incarnation.* (Feel free to go back to Week 1, Day 2 if you need to refresh your memory.)

God came to us in human flesh

Think of some of the Christmas hymns we sing by heart but whose words we may not have given much thought to. Notice the third line of this stanza from Charles Wesley's "Hark the Herald Angels Sing":

Christ by highest heav'n adored, Christ the everlasting Lord;

Late in time behold Him come, Offspring of a Virgin's womb;

Veiled in flesh the Godhead see, Hail the incarnate Deity;

Pleased as man with man to dwell; Jesus, our Emmanuel.[14]

Or what about this line from "O Come, All Ye Faithful":

Word of the Father, now in flesh appearing.[15]

Turn to Hebrews 2:14-17. Why is it important that Jesus became like us in the flesh? List every reason mentioned.

Shared in humanity –
destroy the devil – who holds power over death.

How is both the divinity and humanity of Jesus described in Romans 1:3-4?

human nature like David
HS – declared w power to be the Son of God.
by his resurrection –

I love what Reuben Welch says of the incarnation: "What good is it if Jesus comes to us but he really doesn't come from God? And what good is it if he comes from God but he doesn't really come all the way? He is as much one with us in our humanity, as he is one with the Father in his divinity."[16]

Read Romans 8:1-4 in the HSCB below.

"Therefore, no condemnation now exists for those in Christ Jesus, because the Spirit's law of life in Christ Jesus has set you free from the law of sin and of death. What the law could not do since it was limited by the flesh, God did. He condemned sin in the flesh by sending His own Son in flesh like ours under sin's domain, and as a sin offering, in order that the law's requirement would be accomplished in us who do not walk according to the flesh but according to the Spirit."

No Condemnation
free from Law of Sin &
death.
Condemned Sin in
the flesh –
Law's requirement
for Sin offering.

What did Jesus' coming in the flesh do for us? Again, list everything you see. Respond in the margin.

PERSONAL TAKE: After having now studied 1, 2, and 3 John, why do you think John made such a point of establishing this important doctrine of God coming in flesh right at the top?

We learned earlier in our study that those with gnostic tendencies denied Christ having come in the flesh (an early form of docetism), while others believed in His humanity but not His divinity. The false teachers were trying to separate the divinity of Christ from the humanity of Jesus, but to do this is to miss who Jesus is. And this is why John was so emphatic about it, because to miss Jesus in His wholeness is to miss the Word of Life. A missionary to Ireland wrote: "There was an absolute necessity for Christ to have become one of us. Consider our predicament: we were on earth and God was in heaven. We were polluted, but God was pure. We were unrighteous, but God was just. We needed someone to span the immense divide between God and us and rescue us. But, where could we find someone low enough and high enough all at the same time? The answer was and is in Christ alone."[17]

Where could we find someone low enough and high enough all at the same time?

> Briefly turn to Colossians 2:8-9. Though this is Paul writing, he faced many of the same false doctrines that John was facing. On what were these people basing their beliefs?
>
> *human traditions*
> *Basic Principles of The World.*
>
> How does Paul describe Jesus' divinity and humanity?
>
> *fullness of the Deity Lives in bodily form —*

I can't imagine how anyone could put the reality of the incarnation any better than Welch does here: "What this means is that into your world, your context, your lifestyle—I mean just like it is, just exactly like it is—Jesus comes all the way, and he brings with him the very life of God."[18]

PERSONAL REFLECTION: What part of the incarnation means the most to you and why?

Jesus humanity.

Do you believe this? Really believe it? It's almost easier to dwell on Jesus' divinity because in some ways that keeps Him way "up there" somewhere. But when we dwell on His humanity, He's right here in it with us, and if we're honest this can be a little too close for comfort because we sometimes like to call our own shots.

PERSONAL RESPONSE: In what ways is the incarnation a great comfort to you? In what ways does it disrupt your desire to be in control of your life?

Let's briefly summarize the blessings of believing in the Christ that John had heard, seen, and touched.

1 John 1:3-4.

What gift of community are we given because of Jesus?

Fellowship

1 John 2:1-2.

Who speaks in our defense? Jesus Christ, our ___*defense*___.

He is the propitiation (atoning sacrifice) for our sins. What does this mean? (See Week 2, Day 1 if you need to be reminded.) —

Removal of divine wrath —

1 John 2:20. What do we receive from Jesus, the Holy One?

Truth —

1 John 3:16. What is love and how is Jesus at the center of it?

Laid Down his Life

1 John 4:9-10. How did Jesus show His love to us?

Jesus — atoning sacrifice

1 John 5:13. When we believe in the name of the Son of God we can:
❏ hope we have eternal life.
❏ be in a better position to receive eternal life.
☑ know we have eternal life.
❏ worry and struggle in fear over eternal life.

2 John 9. Whoever continues in the teachings of Christ has both the ___*Father*___ and the Son.

3 John 7. The brothers in the church had gone out sharing the good news in a difficult time for the sake of the ___*Name*___.

As I reflect over John's letters, I'm reminded how impossible this journey would be without Jesus having come to us in the flesh. We have the indicatives: we're forgiven, purified, children of God, overcomers, anointed, and confident that we know. We also have the imperatives: we're to love each other like Christ loved while not loving the world system. Only the incarnation makes both the indicatives and imperatives possible. If all this still feels a little "up there" somewhere, let me put it in the words of one of my favorite hymns, "Crown Him With Many Crowns":

Crown Him the Son of God, before the worlds began,

And ye who tread where He hath trod, crown Him the Son of Man;

Who every grief hath known that wrings the human breast,

And takes and bears them for His own, that all in Him may rest.[19]

Will you turn back to 1 John 1:1-2 one last time in our study together? What parts of these two verses correspond to:

Jesus being the Son of God?

Jesus being the Son of Man?

Jesus came as fully God and fully man (1 John 1-2)

When I think about the incarnation of Jesus—the Son of God (divinity) in human flesh (humanity)—the rest of John's letters fall into place. I still have a lot of questions, now, and a couple of them have caused me to toss around at night. But no unanswered question is greater than the Word of Life who appeared in the flesh: "Who every grief hath known that wrings the human breast." This strikes me at my core every time I sing it. What is the grief that's wrung your heart out? He's felt it, dear sister. What road have you trod that's blistered the soles of your feet? He's tread it, beloved. Where has your shame run so deep that you can't lift your head? He's your Advocate, little child. Who are you struggling to love? He's already shown you how to do it, because He loved you first. Beloved, He's loved you first. "And there is the hope for my world and your world and our great big, wide world."[20]

JOHN'S THEOLOGICAL INGREDIENTS

P. 26

P. 30

P. 34

P. 43

P. 45

P. 52

P. 75

P. 87

P. 89

P. 91

P. 108

P. 111

P. 132

P. 134

P. 137

P. 180.

AUNT ELOTIA'S BLUEBERRY BUCKLE

FROM THE KITCHEN OF AUNT ELOTIA

I came across this recipe on a 3x5 card at a friend's vacation cottage. With the primary ingredient being fresh seasonal blueberries, the date on the card being listed as August 8, 1972, and a name like Elotia, I knew we were on the right track. This dish will exceed your wildest blueberry imaginations. Muffin-like with a light consistency and a sugary top, this will be a new favorite.

MIX TOGETHER:

3/4 cup sugar
1/4 cup soft shortening
1 egg
1/2 cup milk
Sift together & stir in:
2 c flour
2 tsp. baking powder
1/2 tsp. salt

Fold in 2 cups well-drained blueberries.
Pour mixture into greased / floured 8x8 pan.
Sprinkle top with crumb mixture.
Crumb mixture:
1/2 cup sugar
1/3 cup flour
1/2 tsp cinnamon
1/4 cup soft butter
Bake at 375 for 25-35 min.

VIEWER GUIDE

SESSION 7 **KEEP YOURSELVES FROM IDOLS**

#1 Mary _____ at Jesus' feet.

#2 Mary _____ at Jesus' feet.

#3 Mary _____ at Jesus' feet.

GROUP DISCUSSION QUESTIONS:

For you, what in your alabaster jar do you struggle to give to Jesus?

What do you think you are missing about Jesus that Mary of Bethany understood? (Therefore making her want to spill out what was in her jar for Him.)

Why do you think the focus on our idols—trying to stop worshiping them—is so self-defeating?

How can turning our attention to sitting at Jesus' feet, falling at Jesus' feet and worshipping at Jesus' feet be a truer remedy?

In what area(s) of your life do you struggle with the desire to be "first place"? (p. 172)

What has been the single most significant concept of this study for you? (p. 176)

INTRODUCTION

What Love Is: The Letters of 1, 2, 3 John is a video and discussion based Bible study as part of The Living Room Series. The weekly homework along with the teaching videos will promote honest conversation as you study Scripture together. Since conversation is essential to the experience, I've written a few starter questions in both the Listening Guide and Leader's Guide to help get the discussion rolling.

The added recipes encourage groups to eat together because so many great friendships and conversations naturally begin around a dinner table. That said, this study may be used in a variety of large or small group settings including churches, homes, offices, coffee shops or other desirable locations.

TIPS ON LEADING THIS BIBLE STUDY

PRAY: As you prepare to lead *What Love Is* remember that prayer is essential. Set aside time each week to pray for the women in your group. Listen to their needs and the struggles they're facing so you can bring them before the Lord. Though organizing and planning are important, protect your time of prayer before each gathering. Encourage your women to include prayer as part of their own daily spiritual discipline, as well.

GUIDE: Accept women where they are but also set expectations that motivate commitment. Be consistent and trustworthy. Encourage women to follow through on the study, attend the group sessions and engage with the homework. Listen carefully, responsibly guide discussion, and keep confidences shared within the group. Be honest and vulnerable by sharing what God is teaching you throughout the study. Most women will follow your lead and be more willing to share and participate when they see your transparency. Reach out to different ages, backgrounds, and stages of life. This is sure to make your conversation and experience richer.

CONNECT: Stay engaged with the women. Use social media, emails, or a quick note in the mail to connect with the group and share prayer needs throughout the week. Let them know when you are praying specifically for them. Root everything in Scripture and encourage them in their relationship with Jesus.

CELEBRATE: At the end of the study, celebrate what God has done by having your group share what they've learned and how they've grown. Pray together about what commitment God is asking from them as a result of this study.

TIPS ON ORGANIZING THIS BIBLE STUDY

TALK TO YOUR PASTOR OR MINISTER OF EDUCATION: If you're leading this as part of a local church, ask for their input, prayers, and support.

SECURE YOUR LOCATION: Think about the number of women you can accommodate in the designated location. Reserve any tables, chairs, or media equipment for the videos, music, and additional audio needs.

PROVIDE CHILDCARE: If you are targeting moms of young children and/or single moms, this is essential.

PROVIDE RESOURCES: Order leader kits and the needed number of member books. You might get a few extra for last minute sign-ups.

PLAN AND PREPARE: Become familiar with the Bible study resource and leader helps available. Preview the video session and prepare the outline you will follow to lead the group meeting based on the leader helps available. Go to *lifeway.com* to find free extra leader and promotional resources for your study.

EVALUATE

What went well? What could be improved? Did you see women's lives transformed? Did your group grow closer to Christ and to one another?

NEXT STEPS

Even after the study concludes, follow up and challenge women to stay involved with others through another Bible study, church opportunity, or anything that will continue their spiritual growth and friendships. Provide several options of ministry opportunities the members can participate in individually or as a group to apply what they have learned through this study.

WEEK 1

The following suggestions will supplement the discussion starter questions on the viewer guide pages. They are intended to assist you and stimulate discussion.

1. What do you hope to gain from this study and the time spent together?

2. How do you react to the idea that genuine love has substance and definition?

3. Which is most difficult for you to grasp or embrace: Jesus' complete humanity or divinity?

4. John shares "that which was from the beginning." How does the eternal nature of the gospel ground you in a world that is fleeting and temporary?

5. In what ways do you struggle in a culture that often communicates that what a person believes doesn't matter, truth is ever-changing, or the gospel is narrow and confining?

6. How is believing in Jesus a progressive and dynamic process rather than a static past accomplishment?

WEEK 2

For Sessions 2-7 consider beginning each week with an invitation to group members to share from their personal work study by asking the first question below.

1. What was the most impacting moment for you this week? It may be a Bible verse, principle, prayer experience, revelation, new understanding, or conviction.

2. How can you be intentional about giving yourself to Christian fellowship? What keeps you from fellowship (fear, past wounds, insecurity, busyness, selfishness)?

3. Do you primarily look at fellowship from a standpoint of what you can receive, or what you can give? How does this make a difference in your expectations when engaging in Christian relationships?

4. Describe a particularly meaningful time of fellowship

you've experienced. Who encouraged you? How was Christ central to the experience?

5. Did you learn anything new about John's earlier life as a young disciple that surprised you? (Week 1, Day 1)

6. What about Jesus being the Word of Life gives you hope in trying circumstances? (p. 17)

7. What do you appreciate most about the double truth that God is light and in Him is no darkness? (p. 27)

8. Describe a time when you minimized or justified sin in your life? How did this attitude diminish your gratitude for Christ forgiving your sins and cleansing you from all unrighteousness? (1 John 1:9, p. 34)

WEEK 3

1. What was the most impacting moment for you this week (in video or print study)?

2. Turn to Isaiah 5:20 and discuss specific examples in your daily environment of light being cast as darkness and darkness being cast as light. How do you discern what is true darkness and true light?

3. Discuss the relationship between open confession and walking in the light, as well as secret sins and walking in the darkness. Can anyone share a testimony of how bringing a hidden sin or habit to the light has brought you freedom?

4. Kelly spoke of the reality that fellowship with one another is a direct result of walking in God's light (1 John 1:7). How have you seen this play out in your own life where walking in the light of obedience opened up deeper fellowship with others?

5. How has seeing Christ as your Advocate and the propitiation for your sins taken your love and appreciation for Him to a deeper place? (p. 43)

6. John writes about our sins being forgiven as an action that's already been completed through Christ (perfect indicative). At what points in your life do you struggle to believe you really have been forgiven? (p. 57)

7. Loving like Jesus loved is what makes the old command to love others new. How is this both

hopeful and challenging as you seek to love others with the sacrificial love of Christ (1 John 2:7-8)?

8. John warns us about the pride of life, or boasting about what we have and do (1 John 2:15-17). Discuss the difficulties and challenges of staying humble, especially in the realm of social media.

WEEK 4

1. What was the most impacting moment for you this week (in video or print study)?

2. Of the 5 affirmations you noted from the video, which gives you the greatest sense of assurance?

3. How does your understanding of the two types of knowledge, *ginosko* and *eido,* enrich your grasp of what it means to know God?

4. Have you fretted over whether or not you really know God? How did today's teaching give you more confidence? In what areas are you still unsettled?

5. How does the pre-gnosticism that had infiltrated the church of John's day remind you of similar deceptions in current culture?

6. This past week you studied about the secessionists who had left the church. Have you ever wanted to "secede" from the church? If you feel comfortable sharing, what gave rise to this desire and what kept you where you are?

7. What most encourages you about the anointing you have from the Holy Spirit? What about it challenges you most? (p. 75)

8. How have you experienced the Holy Spirit as your teacher? What has He shown you that you otherwise could not have known? (p. 83)

9. What causes you to doubt the validity of God's Word and the guidance of the Holy Spirit? (p. 82) Do you ever feel lured by a "newer" or "more enlightened" belief system? Why or why not?

10. What part of the discussion of *meno/remaining* means the most to you and why? (p. 76)

11. What tempts you to doubt the validity of God's Word and the guidance of the Holy Spirit? (p. 82)

WEEK 5

1. What was the most impacting moment for you this week (in video or print study)?

2. Based on the video and 1 John 2:6, how are you walking as Jesus walked? Where are you keeping in step and what areas could use transformation?

3. Does your daily reality reflect the premise that the pressure is off you and on Jesus as the vine and His Father as the gardener? Or are you constantly striving, fretting and attempting to control?

4. Can you describe a time when the Holy Spirit worked through you in a peaceful, fruit- bearing way as Kelly described? How did this feel distinctly different from striving in your own strength to accomplish something?

5. How have you experienced the truth that obeying God doesn't earn God's love but obedience does allow us to walk more fully in the benefits of His love? (See John 15:9.)

6. How do you relate to the story of Owen?

7. Without being judgmental, how have you been able to "test the spirits" according to John's advice in 1 John 4:1?

8. John writes about love in radical ways. How has your understanding of the way we're to love others deepened and expanded? (p. 110)

9. John wrote that we are overcomers because of Jesus. If you feel comfortable, encourage the group by sharing about something the Lord helped you overcome, something you couldn't have overcome on your own. (p. 107-108)

10. Describe a situation where you distinctly felt different from the world and its desires— where you realized how not-of-this-world you really are. (p. 109)

11. What do you most fear in your relationship with God? (p. 116) How does the fact that the love of God casts out fear bring assurance in your relationship with God? (p. 114-115)

12. How does the word *propitiation* or *atonement* deepen your understanding of God's love for you? (p. 112)

WEEK 6

1. What was the most impacting moment for you this week (in video or print study)?

2. In a culture of countless opinions regarding what love is, how has your definition of love through this study either broadened or narrowed?

3. Describe a time when you gained intimacy with Christ because of a specific act of obedience.

4. Why do you suppose God sometimes demands painful or sacrificial obedience of His children? How have experiences of obedience served as meaningful expressions of how we love God back?

5. What specific truth have you seen this week that encourages you to pray more fervently? (p. 137) In what ways are you encouraged to further give yourself to intercessory prayer?

6. How have you come to a better understanding of the "sin that leads to death"? (p. 142)

7. How has the Holy Spirit rescued you by refusing to let you continue in a specific sin? (p. 144)

8. What means most to you about the reality that Jesus keeps you? (p. 145)

WEEK 7

1. What in your alabaster jar do you struggle to give to Jesus?

2. What does it mean to you that your idols can be made even of good things that have become ultimate things?

3. What do you think you are missing about Jesus that Mary of Bethany understood? (Therefore making her want to spill out what was in her jar for Him.)

4. Why do you think the focus on our idols—trying to stop worshiping them—is so self-defeating? How can turning our attention to sitting at Jesus' feet, falling at Jesus' feet and worshipping at Jesus' feet, be a better remedy?

5. Are you currently struggling with a "Lord if you had been there" moment? If so, how?

6. How was your experience with 2 and 3 John different from 1 John? What aspects or characteristics did you enjoy about these smaller letters?

7. Do you find yourself leaning too far to the "love" side or "truth" side in your relationships? Discuss how you can bring more love or more truth where needed.

8. How would you describe the difference between knowing truth and having it actually dwell inside you? (p. 159)

9. Describe a time when you experienced joy when you saw your "children" walking in the truth. (p. 160)

10. In what area(s) of your life do you struggle with the desire to be "first place"? (p. 172)

11. What has been the single most significant concept of this study for you? (p. 176)

ENDNOTES

WEEK 1

1. Martin Luther, as quoted by Robert W. Yarbrough, *1-3 John* (Grand Rapids, MI: Baker Academic, 2008), 6.
2. A.W. Tozer, *The Pursuit of God* (Camp Hill, PA: Christian Publications, 1993), 69.
3. Stephen S. Smalley, *Word Biblical Commentary*, vol. 51, *1, 2, 3 John* (Revised Edition) (Nashville, TN: Thomas Nelson, 2007), 5.
4. *Ibid.*, 6.
5. Robert W. Yarbrough, *1-3 John* (Grand Rapids, MI: Baker Academic, 2008), 38.
6. Wayne Grudem, *Systematic Theology* (Grand Rapids, MI: Zondervan, 1994), 1245.
7. Yarbrough, *1-3 John*, 36.
8. R. Alan Culpepper, *The Gospel and the Letters of John* (Nashville, TN: Abingdon Press, 1998), 51.
9. I. Howard Marshall, *The Epistles of John* (Grand Rapids, MI: William B. Eerdmans Publishing Company, 1978), 104.
10. Smalley, *Word Biblical Commentary*, 12.
11. John R. Stott, *Tyndale New Testament Commentaries*, Volume 19: *The Letters of John, an Introduction and Commentary*, ed. Leon Morris (Downers Grove, IL: IVP Academic, 1988), 67.
12. Reuben Welch, *We Really Do Need Each Other: A Call to Community in the Church* (Nashville, TN: Generoux Nelson, 1982), 53.
13. John R. Stott, *Tyndale New Testament Commentaries*, 76.
14. Smalley, *Word Biblical Commentary*, 22.
15. Stott, *Tyndale New Testament Commentaries*, 80.
16. Smalley, *Word Biblical Commentary*, 21.
17. Stott, *Tyndale New Testament Commentaries*, 83.

WEEK 2

1. Jeremy Wade, *River Monsters* (Cambridge, MA: Da Capo Press, 2011), 82.
2. Ignacy Sachs, Jorge Wilheim, and Paulo Sérgio Pinheiro, eds., *Brazil: A Century of Change*, trans. Robert N. Anderson (Chapel Hill, NC: The University of North Carolina Press, 2009).
3. Welch, *We Really Do Need Each Other: A Call to Community in the Church*, 75.
4. *HCSB Study Bible* (Nashville, TN: Holman Bible Publishers, 2010), 2235.
5. Smalley, *Word Biblical Commentary*, 44.

6. *Ibid.*, 43.
7. Stott, *Tyndale New Testament Commentaries*, 48.
8. Smalley, *Word Biblical Commentary*, 45.
9. Marshall, *The Epistles of John*, 121.
10. Elizabeth Prentiss, *Stepping Heavenward* (Uhrichsville, OH: Barbour Publishing, Inc., 1998), 29.
11. Smalley, *Word Biblical Commentary*, 39.
12. *Ibid.*
13. Smalley, *Word Biblical Commentary*, 54.
14. Welch, *We Really Do Need Each Other: A Call to Community in the Church*, 17.
15. Stott, *Tyndale New Testament Commentaries*, 99.
16. Stott, *Tyndale New Testament Commentaries*, 101.
17. Smalley, *Word Biblical Commentary*, 77.
18. Marshall, *The Epistles of John*, 142-143.
19. Robert Law, as quoted by Stott, *Tyndale New Testament Commentaries*, 104.

WEEK 3

1. "Dictionaries :: Abide, Abode." *Blue Letter Bible* (online), [cited 21 Aug, 2014]. Available from the Internet: *www.blueletterbible.org/*.
2. "Greek Lexicon :: G3306 (NIV)." *Blue Letter Bible* (online), [cited 21 Aug, 2014]. Available from the Internet: *www.blueletterbible.org*.
3. Smalley, *Word Biblical Commentary*, 112.
4. Stott, *Tyndale New Testament Commentaries*, 116.
5. Smalley, *Word Biblical Commentary*, 113.
6. "Greek Lexicon :: G5545 (NIV)." *Blue Letter Bible* (online), [cited 21 August 2014]. Available from the Internet: *www.blueletterbible.org/*.
7. Smalley, *Word Biblical Commentary*, 118.
8. Stott, *Tyndale New Testament Commentaries*, 24.
9. Smalley, *Word Biblical Commentary*, 120.
10. Welch, *We Really Do Need Each Other: A Call to Community in the Church*, 86.
11. Oswald Chambers, *My Utmost for His Highest* (Uhrichsville, OH: Discovery House Publishers, 1992), 16.
12. *Ibid.*
13. Marshall, *The Epistles of John*, 195.
14. Welch, *We Really Do Need Each Other: A Call to Community in the Church*, 87.
15. *Ibid.*, 88.
16. *Ibid.*, 98.

WEEK 4

1. Yarbrough, *1-3 John*, 208.
2. *Ibid.*, 209.
3. *Ibid.*, 211.
4. Smalley, *Word Biblical Commentary*, 193.
5. Spiros Zodhiates, *The Complete Word Study New Testament* (Chattanooga, TN: AMG Publishers, 1991), 878.
6. *Ibid.*, 965.
7. Marshall, *The Epistles of John*, 204.
8. Yarbrough, *1-3 John*, 224.
9. Marshall, *The Epistles of John*, 205.
10. Zodhiates, *The Complete Word Study New Testament*, 883.
11. Charles Spurgeon, *Morning & Evening* (New Kensington, PA: Whitaker House, 2001), 84
12. Stott, *Tyndale New Testament Commentaries*, 169.
13. Yarbrough, *1-3 John*, 274.
14. Dallas and Melissa Hartwig, *It Starts With Food: Discover the Whole30 and Change Your Life in Unexpected Ways* (Riverside, NJ: Victory Belt Publishing, 2012), 217.
15. Dallas Willard, *Living in Christ's Presence: Final Words on Heaven and the Kingdom of God* (Downers Grove, IL: InterVarsity Press, 2014), 14.

WEEK 5

1. Marshall, *The Epistles of John*, 233.
2. Stott, *Tyndale New Testament Commentaries*, 179.
3. Yarbrough, *1-3 John*, 302.
4. Andrew Murray, *BeliefNet* (online), [cited 21 August 2014]. Available from the Internet: *www.beliefnet.com/quotes*.
5. Yarbrough, *1-3 John*, 307.
6. Marshall, *The Epistles of John*, 251.
7. *Ibid.*, 247.
8. Stott, *Tyndale New Testament Commentaries*, 194.
9. Ken Sande, *The Peacemaker*, Revised and Updated (Grand Rapids, MI: Baker Book House, 2006), 104.
11. Smalley, *Word Biblical Commentary*, 295.

WEEK 6

1. Welch, *We Really Do Need Each Other: A Call to Community in the Church*, 37.

cultivate
A women's gathering around the Word
Featuring
Kelly Minter
Biblically focused and stylistically simple, this gathering offers a time to seek God's Word, worship with an acoustic ensemble, enjoy the warmth of community and prayer, and focus on missional living. If your church or women's ministry is interested in hosting a Cultivate event featuring Kelly Minter, please email info@kellyminter.com or visit Kelly's web site at
www.kellyminter.com

2. Yarbrough, *1-3 John*, 7.

3. C. H. Dodd, as quoted by Smalley, *Word Biblical Commentary*, 306.

4. W. Loader, as quoted by Yarbrough, *1-3 John*, 345.

5. Yarbrough, *1-3 John*, 349.

6. Stott, *Tyndale New Testament Commentaries*, 213.

7. *Ibid.*, 215.

8. Smalley, *1, 2, 3 John*, 331.

9. As quoted by Holly Hanson, "The Dress That Opened Doors," *Women of Faith* (online), 27 March 2013 [cited 21 August 2014]. Available from the Internet: *www.womenoffaith.com*.

10. *HCSB Study Bible* (Nashville, TN: Holman Bible Publishers, 2010), 2237.

11. Yarbrough, *1-3 John*, 386.

12. Stott, *Tyndale New Testament Commentaries*, 235.

13. William Steuart McBirnie, *The Search for the Twelve Apostles* (Carol Stream, IL: Tyndale House Publishers, Inc., 1976), 89.

14. Charles Wesley, George Whitfield, "Hark, the Herald Angels Sing."

15. John Francis Wade, "O Come, All Ye Faithful."

16. Welch, *We Really Do Need Each Other: A Call to Community in the Church*, 31.

17. Miles McKee, "He Became Like Us," *Miles McKee Ministries* (online), 14 May 2014 [cited 15 August 2014]. Available from the internet: *www.milesmckee.com/ww2014.html*.

18. Welch, *We Really Do Need Each Other: A Call to Community in the Church*, 32.

19. Matthew Bridges, Godfrey Thring, "Crown Him with Many Crowns."

20. Welch, *We Really Do Need Each Other: A Call to Community in the Church*, 32.